DANCE
—the sacred art

The *Joy* of *Movement* as *a* Spiritual Practice

Cynthia Winton-Henry

Walking Together, Finding the Way ®
SKYLIGHT PATHS®
PUBLISHING
Woodstock, Vermont

Dance—The Sacred Art:
The Joy of Movement as a Spiritual Practice

2009 Quality Paperback Edition, First Printing
© 2009 by Cynthia Winton-Henry

Unless otherwise indicated, scripture quotations are from the *New Revised Standard Version Bible*, copyright © 1989 by the Division of Christian Education of the National Council of the Churches of Christ in the USA. Used by permission. All rights reserved.

Grateful acknowledgment is given to reprint "A Body Politic of Peace," © 1996 by Gayle Brandeis. It previously appeared in *Heal Your Soul, Heal the World*, June Cotner, ed. (Kansas City, MO: Andrews McMeel Publishing, 1998).

Library of Congress Cataloging-in-Publication Data
Winton-Henry, Cynthia.
Dance—the sacred art : discovering the joy of movement as spiritual practice / Cynthia Winton-Henry.
p. cm. — (The art of spiritual living series)
Includes bibliographical references and index.
ISBN 978-1-59473-268-3 (pbk.)
1. Dance—Religious aspects. 2. Dance—Psychological aspects. 3. Spiritual life. I. Title.
GV1783.5.W55 2009
246'.7—dc22

2009030883

10 9 8 7 6 5 4 3 2 1

Manufactured in the United States of America
Cover Design: Jenny Buono
Cover art: © rgbspace—Fotolia

Walking Together, Finding the Way®
Published by SkyLight Paths Publishing
A Division of LongHill Partners, Inc.
Sunset Farm Offices, Route 4, P.O. Box 237
Woodstock, VT 05091
Tel: (802) 457-4000   Fax: (802) 457-4004
www.skylightpaths.com

Dedicated to Ruth St. Denis,
mystic, pioneer, sacred dancer

For the world and time are the dance of (Love) in emptiness. The silence of the spheres is the music of a wedding feast. The more we persist in misunderstanding the phenomena of life, the more we analyze them out into strange finalities and complex purposes of our own, the more we involve ourselves in sadness, absurdity and despair. But it doesn't matter much, because no despair of ours can alter the reality of things, or stain the joy of the cosmic dance which is always there.... Yet the fact remains that we are invited to forget ourselves on purpose, cast our awful solemnity to the winds and join in the general dance.

—*Thomas Merton*

CONTENTS

INTRODUCTION

THE MOVEMENT OF LIFE

This book is for both newcomers and seasoned movers, for all of us seeking to nourish our connection to the dance of life. The experiential places we will visit in these pages are holy places, yet the only passport needed is a willingness to move, or, as one teacher said, "If not willingness, then willingness to become willing." The means of transport? Dancing the way *you* dance. Codified steps, choreographies, and performance skills are not the superhighway to dancing. Just as breathing is a birthright, so is moving. You already do both all the time.

If you're thinking, "But I'm not a dancer" or "I feel awkward," I hope to reassure you. You don't need a special talent to move. You don't need to be "graceful" or especially coordinated. You don't need a body that's "in shape." I can tell you that after decades of dancing in my spiritual practice, my feet still turn in more than out. I continue to bang into coffee tables and the corners of things, exceed my "ideal weight," and fluctuate between social grace and goofiness. Dancing helps us embrace all this humanity.

Dance connects us to the movement of life. We already know most "secrets" of dancing. The challenge—and gift—is to unlock the amazing wisdom in our bodies. Unfortunately, natural ways to do this have been overlooked and undervalued among "modern people" for such a long time that we may feel as if dancing our own dance is beyond difficult. Yet a wise person said, "If you have faith the size of a mustard seed, you will enter heaven on earth." Mustard seeds are as common in the Middle Eastern plant world as salt and pepper are on the dining room table. Just so, the common mustard seed of dancing is freely available. I'd love to place it in your hands to marvel over.

In the pages of this book, I want to open up the possibilities of dance and movement as a spiritual practice. Perhaps this statement seems like an oxymoron. Some can't quite imagine *dancing* and *spiritual practice* as companions—especially if someone along the way has pointed out the "evils" of dance. Again and again in this book, you will cross the paths of countless people who, whether they intended it or not, heralded dancing as a sacred art. Consider writer and pacifist Aldous Huxley, who once noted, "Movement is so intertwined in the deep order of things that it is with their muscles that humans most easily obtain knowledge of the divine."

Dance is not just a novel way to illustrate beliefs and theology, nor is it dumbed-down prayer. It is a completely different way of knowing the Holy. We need more than words to connect with our Greater Source. Whenever we sit, walk, run, sing, laugh, embrace lovers, gaze at stars, go fishing, and visit trees— all these things involve movement, and they just hint at the divine dance to which we are all invited.

YOUR GUIDE FOR THE JOURNEY

When I go on a journey, I want a guide who knows the terrain. In my memoir, *Chasing the Dance of Life: A Faith Journey*, I wrote, "The dance of life begged me to find it." Looking back, I can now see the benevolent guidance I've received as I danced through my darkest of hours and my most glorious seasons. I'm grateful for the many guides who nudged me to dance, and I'm happy to offer myself to others. Here is a bit of the story of how dancing became central to my spirituality and life practice.

When I was a girl in the Methodist church, Reverend Ray Ragsdale encouraged us kids to sing and dance in youth choir. In spite of old church legacies that viewed dance as a sin, one day he asked me to dance in worship. A veil was lifted. Dancing in church made total sense to me.

When my high school physical education teacher, Mrs. Mac, also began to drop hints about dance in church, I took note. What did she see in me at age sixteen and seventeen? She made a lasting impression on me when, in my senior year, she drove me a hundred miles to meet a minister whose previous life as a professional dancer influenced the life of his congregation. She also encouraged me to enroll as a dance major at UCLA, even though the only dance classes I had taken were the PE dance classes with her in high school.

At UCLA, there was one wintertime that I was hit hard by despair. I couldn't figure out how dance could be of any real use—until I turned to the autobiography of Ruth St. Denis, an early modern dancer who dreamt of a "Church of the Divine Dance." As I read her words in my small Los Angeles apartment, I had a profound religious experience. I felt an unforgettable energy enter my being, and my vision expanded. My heart felt a love so great that all I wanted to do was serve it. When I asked, "How?" I heard my answer.

"Hold dance and religion together."

My work was cut out for me. Curious about dance's untapped power, wisdom, and spiritual technologies, I began researching ways to foster freedom and wholeness in body and soul. Reverend Mike Fink, a campus minister, pointed me to a master of divinity program in theology and the arts at the Pacific School of Religion in Berkeley. There, Judith Rock, Doug Adams, Carla de Sola, and the Sacred Dance Guild showed me that I wasn't crazy. I learned that I was not the only one who sought to understand the role of dance in spirituality.

My dance career began in earnest with the Body and Soul Dance Company where Judith, Phil Porter, and I choreographed, performed in theaters, traveled, and danced in worship. We taught anyone who wanted to learn from us. In our collaboration, I began to recognize movement's uncanny ability to help individuals tap their body wisdom and connect with the Holy.

In 1989, Phil and I founded InterPlay, an active, creative, improvisational approach to unlocking the wisdom of the body through movement, voice, stories, and stillness. As we gently guided people to reconnect with movement and physicality, we began to see folks befriend their natural ability to move. Gradually, we designed a system of practices and tools that reintegrate body, mind, heart, and spirit. We learned that all of us who befriend our natural ability to freely move can quickly grow in intimacy with self, others, the natural world, and God.

Phil and I gradually shaped InterPlay into a set of eight core principles; dozens of incremental, effortless "forms" of practice; and twenty-six tools. Most of the ideas and practices I will be sharing in this book are taken from InterPlay, which has now become a worldwide organization of teachers, movers, leaders, and "players." I am humbled and amazed that, like those whom we have taught, Phil and I also use the InterPlay tools as the cornerstone of our own spiritual practice. It is our reference for living healthy, happy, creative, and grace-filled lives. I believe we deliberately yet mysteriously stumbled onto a landscape known to many dancers, shamans, and artists. Today, when I hit big speed bumps and obstacles in life, I rejoice that I have a way to get quick, efficient help from the wisdom of the body.

While my religious upbringing is Christian, as I chased the dance of life across the United States and with people in Europe, West Africa, Australia, and India, I couldn't help but open my heart to diverse worldviews. People everywhere became my teachers. Perhaps I am more of an amateur anthropologist than a theologian. My approach to art and spirituality is characterized by inquisitiveness and philosophical research into the role of sacred imagination and the biomechanics of transformation that lurk behind most cultural theories about Spirit. As a consequence, though I claim the Christian taproot of my family tree, my faith has multiple branches and twigs of spiritual practice. Buddhists, Jews, Pagans, and Mayans teach me; Africans, American Indians, Aboriginal Australians, and Indians influence me. Dancing taught me that the common soil, sun, and air of our physicality unite us. I am grateful to live in a place and time when all these resources are literally at my doorstep and fingertips.

Having benefited from so many teachers, guides, therapists, and friends, I now recognize that very few people venture down spiritual paths alone. We need support from teachers and spiritual directors. At the back of this book, you'll find resources pointing to potential support for dance and spirituality in your area. They can be found in dance therapy contexts, religious and liturgical dance groups, the Sacred Dance Guild, the Contact Improvisation network, Conscious Dance's online directory, theater groups, groups like InterPlay, or listed on the board at your local grocery store. Practitioners of t'ai chi, yoga, aikido, and martial arts are dance's first cousins. They offer similar experiences, too.

People around you are moving. Anyone who googles *dance* alongside words such as *ecstatic, worship, meditation, somatic, trance,* and *praise* will uncover a network of seekers actively embracing the moving arts as a way to connect to Spirit. The field of dance and spirituality is growing. If you are new to it, consider this book as your personal invitation to join in the dance.

INVITATION TO DANCE

Just as I have welcomed many other newcomers walking through the door, ready to explore dance as part of their spiritual path, I welcome you. This book is written in honor of the You who sits in the chair or crouches by a bookshelf, the You who senses that dance might be more than a recreational activity. This book is *not* about winning the "Soul Celebrity Dance-Off." It's not an ab-tightening spiritual fitness program. It is about rekindling the power and joy in your creative connection to the dancing universe. It's about soul power.

Vinn Marti, creator and minister of Soul Motion, once said, "The hardest part is over. You're here. Whatever it took to make the journey from the outside world, whatever obstacles you had to overcome are behind you. It's over, it happened, you're here. I invite you to come down from the tower of thought and enter the heart of humanity."

You're here. You are holding this book in your hand. You have your innate ability to move. You are ready. Let the reflections and practices in this book draw you into the river of dance. Splash around in these pages as you like, or jump in and read it straight through.

I invite you to take a moment to breathe and pray in your own way or with me:

O movement of life,
your waters are holy.
Bless us in these contemplations
as we enter your tributaries, rivers, and seas,
preparing to immerse every cell in grace and truth.
Teach us again how to begin the dance,
moving from moment to moment
and day to day.

A DANCING PARABLE *

Once upon a time a woman grew quite sad. Her stomach grumbled and churned as if it were always complaining. She tried everything she knew—medicine, distraction, love, bearing and raising children. Nothing gave her ease. Finally, she went to the village wise woman and asked, "What am I to do?"

"Have you listened to the voices in your belly?" the wizened one asked.

"Listen to them?"

"Yes, those voices in the belly will speak to us if we will only listen. Would you like me to help you listen?"

At first the woman was unsure, but she was so tired of the churning in her belly, what did she have to lose? She consented.

Together they sat in the quiet. After quite a while, she felt a nest of restless, squirming, yellow-belly snakes all bunched up in her guts. Suddenly, a voice screamed, "SING! DANCE! YOU MUST SING OR WE WILL EAT YOU!"

She jumped, terrified and surprised to hear a voice holler out of nowhere. She looked at the wise woman, who only nodded and shrugged. "There's your answer."

"Sing my song? What song?"

The old woman said, "You must find it for yourself."

*Adapted by Cynthia Winton-Henry from *Yellow Belly Snakes* (unpublished) by Dori Joyner.

The woman was scared of snakes and even more anxious about yellow-belly snakes that speak. Not wanting to be eaten, she felt she had no choice but to listen. She immediately began traveling to all the local villages to learn songs, wondering which one was hers. In her travels she discovered that learning and singing songs did ease the churning in her belly. After several years, having learned all the songs that there were to learn, she sat down and rested by a tree. Suddenly, the snakes started churning as ferociously as ever. Startled and upset, this time she talked directly to them: "Snakes! Why are you still churning? I've sung all the songs! Hundreds of them, in fact."

"BUT YOU HAVE NOT SUNG OUR SONG OR DANCED OUR DANCE! DO IT OR WE'LL NOT ONLY EAT YOU, WE'LL EAT YOUR CHILDREN!"

Terrified, she ran home as fast as she could to check on her children. Seeing them safe in bed, she took a deep breath, much relieved. Lying down with them, she fell asleep. In the morning the eldest child rolled over, tugged at her chin, and complained, "Mommy, it hurts."

"What? What hurts?" she asked, still full of sleep.

"Churning, snaky pain, fighting in my tummy," said the child.

Her eyes froze open, pinned on her child.

She was devastated. What was she to do? She went out into the forest and began to wail. Her cries were loud and long at first. Her body rose and fell with weeping. Eventually, the cries turned to moans. "Snakes, snakes, snakes," she said over and over in a self-hypnotizing rhythm.

"*Yes!*" whispered the snake.

The woman stopped. What had she heard?

"Don't stop," said the yellow-belly snakes.

The woman took a deep breath. Exhaling, she let her voice and body continue to move.

"*Yes! Yes!*" said the snakes. The snakes moved within her. The more they moved, the more the tightness loosened.

Relieved, the woman moaned and sang and danced until she could move and speak no more. Finally, she rested.

Days went by, and months. Neither her stomach nor her children's knew any discomfort. Then, a year to the day, her stomach clenched up. She heard the snakes scream, "*Dance! Sing!*" She was shocked. She had forgotten the song that she sang before.

"I don't remember the song," she trembled.

"Sing us our song!" demanded the snakes. She stood up and took a deep breath in. As she exhaled out came a long, wavery tone. One after another. The sound was thin at first but gradually opened into a series of vibrating notes. As she sang, she remembered to dance as her hips and belly moved. The song was completely different.

"Yes," said the snakes. "That's our song, that is our dance, new every moment. Thank you."

From that day forward, the woman danced and sang frequently. When her friends asked her what she was doing, she told them that she was feeding her snakes and invited them to join. Her children learned to do this, too.

CHAPTER ONE

MAY I HAVE THIS DANCE?

"I would believe only in a God that knows how to dance."

—*Friedrich Nietzsche*

The Divine, holding out a hand like a lover or an old friend, eyes expectantly on us, utters five golden words: "May I have this dance?"

Though we feel as if we are nothing but elbows and knobby knees, we can't resist. We take one step toward the Great Dancer, holding our breath, certain the next words will be, "So you think you can dance?"

Instead, the Holy moves with us, matching us so perfectly that each pulse, sway, and point of pressure that we apply is validated as perfect. We've never moved with such grace.

One Sunday morning, at the end of a weekend workshop, I invited people to dance in relationship with the One-They-Turn-To. For fifteen minutes there was only music, morning light, and bodies alternately moving and sinking into stillness. A woman who had just lost her rabbi to a tragic drowning felt her dancing salve her grief. A seventy-year-old Episcopal priest let joy guide her after years of fighting for human rights. A man preparing to marry his beloved let his heart open wider. A bereaved woman drained by care for her mother refreshed herself in the healing waters of movement. An astrophysicist who has studied the birth of stars remembered the mystery of her own body. When the dance was over, their faces were radiant and peaceful. There is nothing I love more than companioning people who are discovering movement as a spiritual practice.

At the beginning of nearly every culture, dance arose at the foundation of collective spiritual life. Just as inconceivable as separating out deities and goddesses from everyday activities, dancing was intrinsic to the religiosity of indigenous groups. It could not be extricated. It was manna, daily bread. More than mere expression, dancing served as the primary means of knowing and creating the world. It carried technologies of healing, entertainment, and most definitely of praying.

Those who study Judaism and the Bible discover that dancing is embedded in the fabric of worship, language, and Jewish ritual. From the beginning, God *moved* over the face of the deep, psalms were sung with timbrel and dance, and prophets like Isaiah declared, "You shall go out with joy and be led forth in peace: The mountains and the hills shall break forth into singing, and all the trees of the field clap their hands" (Isaiah 55:12). Dancing has always allowed the Transcendent to move among us.

One of my favorite examples of dancing hidden in these sacred texts is found in the Hebrew word for festival, *hagag*, meaning "to move in a circle." Jewish festivals and High Holy Days include circle dancing, not as an afterthought or an add-on to the important parts of ceremony, but as sacred containers into which the spiritual truths of community were reliably and regularly sealed, revealed, and renewed. Not to dance would be like not worshipping.

So, too, for the first Christians. Did Jesus dance? His presence at the wedding at Cana, his description of rejoicing at the reunion of the prodigal son, which included the instruction to kill the fatted calf and make merry, his instruction "to rejoice and leap for joy" (Luke 6:23)—these put him in the thick of dancing. And if he himself didn't dance, certainly the earthy prostitutes, fishing people, and commoners who followed him performed dance, storytelling, and song as some of their few creative outlets.

Because dance isn't written down, there are scant records of its pervasiveness. But that doesn't mean it wasn't playing a central role. From observing cultures around the world, I tend to think that dance was such a common, collective prayer form that no one would ever imagine that it could become endangered. No one ever thought, "We need to protect the dance, make laws like 'Thou shalt dance.'" Dancing is joy's natural expression. To inhibit it is to inhibit the love of God.

Indigenous Europeans, like other tribal people, also related to their gods and goddesses through dancing. When individuals, households, and cultures increasingly converted to Christianity, they continued to hold onto their dances. We know this because there are records of church leaders who resisted the peasant dances done in churches and churchyards, dances undoubtedly laden with the lived experience, symbolism, and values of the ancient earth-based religions. In addition, there is evidence of dances that successfully contributed to cathedral pageants—as a means of mourning or to support healing, like during the plagues in the "Dances of Death"—as well as tales of musicians, actors, and dancers who served as minstrels and jesters, wandering from place to place to teach people about life.

When I discovered that *carol* means "to dance," and *chorus* relates to *choreo* and *choreograph*, meaning "to dance together," I realized that our European Christmas carols and choruses sprang right from the festive dance. And, when my friend Judith Rock did her doctorate on Jesuit ballet in Paris in the Baroque period, a time of intellectual and artistic development that inspired theater as we know it, I was exposed to dance's role in teaching people about humanist values. Performing in the reconstruction of one of these ballets at St. Ignatius of Loyola Catholic Church in San

Francisco, I discovered that intellectualism, reason, humor, piety, and faith when embodied in dancing were not always at odds.

Dancing, it seems, is inherent in the root system of the Christian family tree.

How disturbing, then, that something as prayerful, joyous, and revelatory as movement could so severely atrophy among a people who celebrate a God described as "at home in flesh" and "at one" with a creation resplendent with beauty and grace. I can't tell you how many people have shown up at workshops and classes looking for reconnection with their bodies. I have to ask, "What got in the way of our freedom to move, to dance?" While there is a movement to reclaim Christianity and other Western traditions as dancing faiths, some religious leaders still seem determined to prohibit dancing. Why?

FOUR MYTHS

While dancing can bring great joy, it is, unfortunately, considered "dangerous" by some people. One priest even described a group of youth dancing in Catholic worship as "spiritual terrorists." Protestant culture, in particular, has a history of relegating dance to murky corners, along with cards, gambling, and drinking. Even chaperoned junior high sock hops were spiritually suspect. Old prohibitions stifle dance to this day. As poet John Masefield, in honor of English dancers, once cried out, "Dance was despised and held in shame/Almost something not to name."

And it is not only religious cultures that inhibit dance. Religious anxiety about the body seems to perfectly sync up with the timing of the onset of industrialization and colonization. Wanting to believe that commercial prosperity would bring happiness and alleviate suffering, a lot of people became cogs in the industrial machine. As they did, their folk songs, stories, and dances diminished like endangered species. Decade after decade, as the new, industrialized, civilized, "progressive" values spread to other continents, they began to devastate many of the world's dancing cultures. Indigenous leaders like the Northern Plains shaman Wovoka, who dreamt and created the Sun Dance, saw the effects of this and warned his people, "All Indians must dance, everywhere, keep on dancing. Pretty soon in next spring, Great Spirit come.... Indians who don't dance ... will grow little, just about a foot high, and stay that way." Losing sight of the goodness of the body and dancing caused the likes of Jewish theologian Martin Buber to state the obvious: "The soul is not really united unless all the bodily energies, all the limbs of the body are united."

Immigrants from dancing cultures are co-opted by this colonizing "de-dancification" even today. I will never forget the sad, bewildered expression on one Indian man's face when he noticed his reluctance to dance while attending a festival in his homeland. "Didn't I used to enjoy dancing?" he wondered. A successful professional, he hadn't realized how much he'd disinherited his joyous, dancing culture.

After decades of teaching dance, I've witnessed the dramatic effects of this antidance, body-distanced sentiment. Students who have taken any of my classes on dance in relation to theology, prayer, healing, activism, or death and dying often report that their weekly visits are the most difficult, yet transformational experiences, of their education—not because they couldn't do the things being asked of them, but because they had to confront levels of love, freedom, and joy so easily accessible. As soon as they started to dance, they sensed strange, almost miraculous possibilities as well as formidable hindrances. Many of these people who felt called to ministry had to face the power (or, as the Buddhists would say, "illusions") of their unruly wills, poor body image, limited imaginations, and lagging marks in the "fun department." With nothing but love and affirmation coming from others—and me—they had to ask themselves why *wouldn't* they want to engage and share their spontaneous, embodied, soulful selves.

Teaching methods used in schools and religious centers reinforce the split between body, mind, heart, and spirit. "Sit still. Line up. Don't move. Stop squirming. Pay attention. Focus on the board. Head down. Don't touch that. Do your work. Stop playing." Habituated patterns in our movements are so tightly woven into how and what we think and do that we readily perpetuate numerous myths about why we can't and won't dance. In this system those who excel at quiet focus succeed. Those who need to move are considered less bright. Everyone loses. The same conditions occur in religious community, and they perpetuate four myths that stop us from being able to let go and move.

MYTH 1: IT'S TOO EMBARRASSING TO DANCE

It's true that a lot of us are self-conscious. Dancing can put us on the spot. When we are shy, awkward, or get shamed for not knowing which foot to use and which way to turn, it is easy to convince ourselves that it is too late for foolishness like dance. Yet, we can also amaze ourselves. "The young shall see mighty visions, and the old shall dream dreams," says Spirit in Acts 2:17. What if you don't have to know your left from your right to do a duet with God?

Just on the other side of the speed bump of embarrassment, you might take the vow of that great dancer, Snoopy, who said, "If you can't dance, you should at least be able to do a happy hop." Embarrassment happens, but it is not coming from God.

I am committed to doing everything in my power to make the speed bumps of self-consciousness as minimal as possible. If the chance of embarrassment is decreased to a 2 or 3, on a scale of 1 to 10, most people will at least consider giving dance a try.

MYTH 2: THERE IS NO CONNECTION BETWEEN DANCE AND SPIRITUALITY

If you talk casually to most Western people, you'll most likely find that they think it odd to put dance and spirituality together. Talking to groups, I get a laugh when I say that; for a while, my job was to put dance and the ministry together. Having sashayed down church aisles only to be later confronted by religious elders who told me to stop, I know this dichotomy well.

We may have managed to squeeze movement out of our houses of worship, yet many people delight in remembering weddings and ceremonies when people danced, lifted each other up in procession, and celebrated.

Dance still thrives in many "minority" groups. Those who have eyes to see will note this. Those who look only through the small lens of words and ideas may not. One story is told of an American philosopher visiting a Shinto priest who said, "We've been now to a good many ceremonies, and I have seen quite a few of your shrines, but I don't get your ideology. I don't get your theology." The Japanese priest paused and then slowly shook his head. "I think we don't have ideology," he said. "We don't have theology. We dance."

If embodiment is the practice of making our experience physically real and visible, then what would your "theology of embodiment" look like? If your faith recognizes the human body as a temple, is yours a temple of beauty, joy, and grace? Could this living temple arise in something as easy as taking a walk or letting breath, heart, and cadence move you? Does the Divine move with your rising and falling? Even though we may not see the dance in our lives, the connection is still there.

MYTH 3: THE BODY IS PANDORA'S BOX AND NOT TO BE TRUSTED

This may be the most troubling myth of all. It's one that we unknowingly inherit from long lines of relatives and elders who equated dance with the work of the devil and held it in "ill repute." It is a historical fact that religious elites and conquerors from Europe and North America repeatedly outlawed and suppressed dance. The founding fathers of the New World were religious reformers and politicians whose work ethic and social order promoted the pursuit of happiness through productivity, reason, and piety. To this day, American citizens are known to be socially friendly and yet inhibited at school, in worship, and in "business mode." Moving, breathing aloud, laughing, touching, and loving each other are for "recreation only."

At the other extreme, we have gregarious bar dances, pregame rowdiness, and concerts full of crazed and drunken dancers whose activities confirm the myth that the body is not to be trusted. As a humorous sign says, "Alcohol: Helping white people dance for hundreds of years."

Human experience is complex and temptations are mighty. But suppression is a harsh blanket to throw over such colorful lives. It smothers everything. Why not consider the wisdom of Uruguayan writer Eduardo Galeano: "The Church says: The body is a sin. Science says: The body is a machine. Advertising says: The body is a business. The Body says: I am a fiesta." *Olé!*

The body is not a bedeviled box; it's a theater of truth. Our job is not to discourage life or truth, but to offer it up to love and, as much as possible, create beauty in it. A spiritual path teaches us to choose joy, kindness, love, and healing. This is hard to do underneath a thick, heavy, darkened shroud. To do this we need permission, discipline, and support.

MYTH 4: DANCING ISN'T IMPORTANT

It's true. Dancing can get so buried under the laundry of life's dos and don'ts that it barely appears as a desire, much less a form of spirituality. Yet on a daily basis, dance tugs at our sleeves. She makes us pick up that brochure about a class until we finally put it on the fridge. She whispers, "Remember how it felt to move freely?" One day we put aside all our lists. We take the class. We begin to recall that dancing is more important than laundry and appointments.

This is why on Monday morning in the InterPlay studio, a dozen or more women faithfully gather. Many are over fifty years old. Pat and Susan are in their eighties. Some of these women say that this community is critical to their well-being. So much so that Pat decided *not* to move to another city to be near her grandkids, and Susan, who moved to the area to be closer to family, made it her priority to find this particular group.

Too busy? I've seen people who are so parched for dance that even a small sip of it is like an elixir. Like ascetics who fast from food and drink for long periods in order to heighten sensitivity to the whispers of divine love, these newcomers, who have often unknowingly refrained from dancing their prayers, find that even a small experience of divine grace through simple movement feels acute, imbued with the power of grace.

Dancing not important? I remember the first time I heard, "I don't have a body, I *am* my body." What a revelation! There is a yearning in us to be known, to let the body speak, to remember that movement as a sacred art can reconnect us with ourselves, bring us together, and lead us to the Divine. Rather than being a luxury or a specialty for a limited few, dancing is a vital force that reweaves our dynamic wholeness as both individuals and communities.

Some say such dancing saved their lives. Though dancing needn't be that important to be beneficial, sometimes it undeniably is.

❖ ❖ ❖

Today we are slowly beginning to set aside these entrenched myths. In higher education, theories of embodiment and integrated forms of inquiry are brewing and taking shape. Research is confirming the productivity of whole-brain activity. Instead of denigrating or condemning dance, many are choosing more freedom of movement, following in those footsteps of Emma Goldman, influential and well-known anarchist, who quipped, "If I can't dance, I don't want to be part of your revolution."

If some of these myths fit things you've been taught or believe, this is a chance to join the movement that John Masefield was alluding to in his poetry. Dance may have been "despised and held in shame," "but up the lovely flower came."

FOUR ENCOURAGEMENTS

If you're wondering how dancing can make such a difference without years of instruction, I can tell you that, over and over again, I've seen how simple movement practices lead to great renewals in spirit-centered living. Whether you've danced for years or barely moved, the rituals of dance can and do foster wisdom. There are four encouragements, in particular, that I offer those I teach—and you. They won't make you into a professional dancer or automatically release latent kinesthetic tendencies, but these encouragements lay out the welcome mat for your dancing life.

ANYONE CAN DANCE

As I improvise a dance with Nicole, a mature woman with Down's syndrome, she blesses me. She literally takes my cheeks and head in her hands to kiss me on the forehead and then transitions with open arms and well-placed movement to someone else in the room who will receive a similar danced blessing. She has danced, with the support of her mom, Marvel, her whole life. Marvel and Nicole frequently dance, play, perform, and pray together.

Megan, a social worker in a wheelchair named "Stella," zooms across the floor like an angel. Muscular dystrophy prohibits her arms from lifting in the air, but it has not inhibited her from being a virtuoso in the dance of life. Transferring from bed to chair, she uses every bit of her dance awareness to make each movement count as a sacred act. She is an Olympian of the spirit and a soul mate in the dance company we're both in.

A lack of endurance, grace, youth, or confidence does not deter these women from dancing! On the contrary, movement elevates their emotional, physical, and psychic intelligence to transcendent places, even when their words, ideas, and body parts aren't well formed. Whether you are trained or new to movement as a spiritual practice makes no difference. It's not the way you dance that matters; it's something deeper, something that rises from a willingness and intention that liberates the Source of Knowing within you. That is where the dance resides.

THERE IS NO RIGHT WAY TO DANCE

In his book *Real Christians Don't Dance,* writer John Fisher speaks of the offbeat spontaneity of faith and dance: "It's not always pleasing to the eye, but [the Spirit of God's] dance is fresh.... It isn't well rehearsed, polished, or perfect; it slips and slides, sometimes innovative and shocking and at other times just exhilarant, but it's always real."

Is there a "right way" to be a soul? Our souls are like gorgeous, wild, highly intuitive creatures. We wouldn't tell a tiger, "Don't haunch like that," or say to a bird, "Hey, you need to use more extension in your wings." We don't tell the sun to move a little to the left, or request a redwood to stand up straighter. Thank heaven that animals and the rest of creation don't have to carry the burdens of self-consciousness that we do. The animals would be falling all over themselves.

The "right way" to dance is to dance *you.* The challenge is to create or find the safety that allows you to find out what this means. When people allow their original ways of moving to come with ease and joy, they exude an observable power that others can often see. I call this essence "bodyspirit." *Bodyspirit,* similar to the term *bodymind* used by mindfulness practioners, intentionally combines *body* and *spirit* to reinforce and remind us that our human soul is inherently embodied as long as we are alive.

When I think of bodyspirit, I picture Martha Graham. She was not only an icon in the dance world, who engaged every cell of her being in conversation with the great myths of Western culture, she was fierce in her commitment to life. As such, she implored fellow choreographer Agnes DeMille in a letter with these words:

"There is vitality, a life force, a quickening that is translated through you into action, and because there is only one of you in all time this expression is unique. And if you block it, it will never exist through any other medium, and be lost. The world will not have it. It is not your business to determine how good it is; nor how valuable it is; nor how it compares with other expressions. It is your business to keep it yours clearly and directly, to keep the channel open." I believe she was referring to what I call bodyspirit.

Your dance grows from following *your* energy, *your* individual curiosity about experience, and *your* intentions. Your bodyspirit has its own agenda, its own vocabulary, and its own necessary communications. During my two decades of leading small groups of people into dance, I have never seen it fail that when people become unified—body and soul—and receive assurance that these expressions will not only be accepted but will also benefit others, they become grateful and enthusiastic proponents of it. It's as if they knew what was in them all along and, like kids looking at the gifts under a Christmas tree, had to wait for that one bright morning to finally open them.

All you have are my words of assurance to "dance the way *you* dance." But I do know the power of dance, and I pray that you will find the support you need to do this. Oddly, when you do, I think you'll find that it's the most natural thing in the world. You'll even wonder what the big deal was all about.

DANCE CAN CHANGE YOUR LIFE

When writer Naomi Steinfield described her life before she started dancing, she lamented her awkwardness: "For thirty-nine years I was a klutz. The kind who bumps into tables. Navigating through a restaurant was hard enough—I was not about to take dance classes and thereby suffer the humiliation of probing my body's ineptitude right out there in public. So I didn't. I spared myself that pain. Instead I suffered the greater pain of hungering for a gracefulness that was clearly beyond my reach."

Then one dance class changed her life. Naomi was invited to a class taught by Katharine Harts, who welcomed Naomi into her own movement and taught her that "right" is irrelevant: "When you can feel the inner quality of your own particular body ... you dance as a conversation with yourself.... And in this state of self-harmony, you are no longer a collection of separate, disorganized body parts. *You ... are dance.*"

Dancing activates the living waters within us. I know this from personal experience and from witnessing it. Dance can help us find God, access wisdom, and recover our souls. In many cases, dance can be the healer that carries us over troubled terrain and rescues us from "the pit."

I think of my friend Soyinka, statuesque and powerful, whom I met when she played a plaintive, improvised Native American flute melody for an event I was leading. Over time, I learned that while she was growing up, her brother had been murdered and her mom had died from a crippling disease. Yet, through movement, breath, leading kids in yoga, and prayer, she had found enough solace to stay alive. Beyond that, she eventually created a home studio, making a sanctuary of her space as she constantly extends invitations to people to come dance, sing, drum, breathe, and reconnect to love. She calls the necessary work she does "Our Thing."

Many people say that life is change. One of the most significant ways we can transform our experience and worldview is to join with this ever-changing reality. The idea of dancing our lives can elevate our relationship to change as we choose to embody each evolving, new pattern and pathway. Dancing helps us move from form to form. That is "trans-formation," something each of us can learn to do with increased grace and ease.

A ONE-HAND DANCE

I often joke that it's countercultural to raise your arms up over your head. Look around. Do you see anyone on the street or at the office with his arms in the air? Something even that simple demands that we rewire our collective body agreements. When I introduce dance movements, I find that this "rewiring" happens rather easily when I focus on things anybody can do. Simple movements clear away mental clutter and ideology, help people bow to the moment, shake out, warm up, and connect to life's flow.

How does the dance begin? It can start with a deep breath—or even one hand. Let me introduce you to this simple one-hand dance. My codirector at InterPlay, Phil Porter, says in his playful book *The Slightly Mad Rantings of a Body Intellectual: Part One,* "Almost everyone's hands dance without effort or awareness. They take off like startled birds almost every time words slip from our lips.... We teach people to do it because we have discovered that almost everyone can do it.... If you are willing to follow the movement of your hand and hang out with it long enough, you will be transported."

Limiting our dance to one hand allows extraordinary freedom to occur. In a sneaky way, it disables ego, vanity, and fear. Playing with a humble hand is like turning the key in the ignition of whole-body intelligence and firing the engine that can take us to multidimensional places that thoughts alone rarely access. As one InterPlay participant put it, "Normally I would be much more self-conscious about doing this. [But] to have a hand dance, where that is all that I need to worry about, greatly opens things up. It makes the playing field small and safe, so I can truly begin to 'be in movement,' without thinking or trying or worrying."

I have done many, many of these one-hand dances. Lying on my back, I raise a hand in the air. Listening to the music, my eyes relax and my hand takes on a life of its own. For a minute my body isn't something to feel good or bad about. My body is me. I am movement. I'm not performing. Am I praying? Meditating? Dancing? Discerning? On vacation? In minutes I feel more at peace. Could serenity be so possible? Could help be a mere movement away?

Would you like to give it a try? You might begin by putting on music, placing one hand in the air, and letting it move like seaweed. But don't trust my words; try it for yourself. Don't try to force any particular postures; simply let this extension of your body move.

One-Hand Dance

With or without music, invite the dance of one hand. For ten seconds each:

~ Move your hand in smooth ways.
~ Move your hand smooth and fast.
~ Move it in jerky ways.
~ Move it jerky and slow.
~ Let your hand make a shape.
~ Make other shapes.
~ Make contact with your skin.
~ Feel free to let go of making meaning.
~ Enjoy any sensations, thoughts, textures, dynamics, and nuance as you move any way you like.
~ When you come to an ending, take a deep breath. What do you notice?

❖ ❖ ❖

Twelfth-century mystic Meister Eckhardt said, "The soul loves the body." When you honor your soul's deep intimacy with your physicality, you create space for Great Love to reside in you. If you are willing to grab hold of the divine hand that is constantly extending itself to you and step onto the easygoing, forgiving floor that supports the dance of life, you may come to ask, as many do, "Why did I wait so long?"

CHAPTER TWO

APPROACHING HOLY GROUND

"When you commit to a movement, you make it with your whole body. When you commit to a feeling, your passion will give power to your message. When you commit to a dance, your feeling reaches beyond your limitations."

—Aziza Sa'id, dancer

When you play music, do you tap your foot? Feel a pulse? Sway? It's no surprise. The dancing universe is literally in us. One hundred twenty-five billion chains of DNA are spiral-dancing inside our bodies. These little turnkeys unlock vast amounts of knowledge hidden from the mind and on infinitesimal levels connect us to the ancient dance of our human ancestors. Our cells vibrate with movement. Gerardus Van Der Leeuw writes in *Sacred and Profane Beauty,* "Dance is not something in which we can participate or not as we like. Whoever does not dance runs races, waddles, limps—that is, they dance badly. We must all learn once more to dance."

When was the last time you rolled on the floor, leaned on a companion, ran around a room, whooped, or sang freely for no good reason? When was the last time you sighed out loud, cried, laughed, moaned, or did a jig of elation? Even our fear wants to dance. Watch a person in pain. They rock. In mourning or joy, the dance of life wants to sweep us off our feet and onto the next stage.

Even people with the courage to show their abandon need places of love and permission. That is what sanctuaries are for. Every dancer needs a sanctuary. Lacking one, we may need to create a conscious space for ourselves that says, "Yes! Dance is a way to communicate with God."

How shall we make way for the sacredness of our own dance? What supports are needed if we long to be moved by the Holy?

BOWING TO THE DANCE

Sometimes the wisdom of the body spontaneously nudges us toward health and wholeness. It caused Julie, while writing down her doubts and fears about life in her journal, to suddenly scrawl in large letters, "SHUT UP AND DANCE!" This surprised her so much that she had to listen.

Something that lives beyond ordinary thought and action may ignite our reverential reflex toward sacred dance. That "something" nudged Pat, a respected church elder who was on her way to becoming a Baptist minister. One day, while signing up for seminary classes, she heard God say, "Now go dance," and thought, "For heaven's sake, I can barely kneel." She signed up for a class on dance and prayer in spite of herself and never regretted it.

Most of us take our first steps onto the Divine's sacred dancing ground with less theatricality. Notice movements you already make. Might not they be sacred? Sometimes joy and communion sneak up on us through everyday motions, like sweeping or raking or walking. In the midst of common movement, grace can awaken a surprising sense of meaning. A sensation of "being danced" might glisten like gold on the surface of our consciousness as our cells interconnect with a greater pattern of meaning.

C. S. Lewis clues us into this in his novel *Perelandra*: "In the plan of the Great Dance plans without number interlock, and each movement becomes in its season the breaking into flower of the whole design to which all else had been directed." Is this poetry or reality? Mystics find it hard to differentiate between the two.

Anna, a grandmother in North Carolina, brings us a bit closer to understanding our potential intimacy with the Great Dance in her reflections: "I was witness to the spring leaves dancing in my backyard this past week. They were shimmering in their play between shadow and sunlight, moved by a gentle breeze. I knew these new green leaves were embodying the physicality of Grace, just as my friend Lorrie dances with such beauty and grace!"

So, too, does Adyashanti, a contemporary North American Buddhist, who wrote in *Emptiness Dancing*, "There is a saying in Zen, 'When the realization is deep, your whole being is dancing.'"

What is it like to be a devotee dancing before a shrine or a worshipper bowing to receive communion? At times, the movement of the sacred is so interior we feel it only in hidden places within. Yet our body wisdom sometimes longs to reach beyond our ordinary self to reunite with Mystery. Our arms lift and our head is thrown back in a full consent to the Dance of Life.

An ancient saying of Jesus in the Greek Gospel of Thomas proclaims, "Raise the stone, and there you will find me; cleave the wood, and there I am" (30). In response to the Numinous that seems to move people all around the planet, from the high mountains of Tibet to the fields of Poland, we instinctively and ritually honor divine incarnations with basic bows and the honesty of arms lifted. The simple act of bowing is where many a sacred movement begins and ends. Consciously or unconsciously, when we bow our heads, we submit to something greater, our heart comes closer to earth in surrender. When we lift our hearts and hands, we prepare ourselves to greet a "body" that is bigger than our own flesh. "Come home," says this more expansive, inclusive body, which the Greeks called the *soma*.

Such whole and holy gestures help us respond to the Great Sacredness encountered in the earth and sky—and our bodies. Our bodies are not mere hardware boxes of organic circuitry. As we begin to listen to what the body knows and reinclude movement as a starting point for sacred connection, we unlock a much bigger sense of connectional reality. Oneness is not merely an attitude; it's physical.

Movement is part of us. In some ways, we barely need to prepare. The Holy may have already invited us to dance, or we may be just realizing that dance could be the best bet for making a date with a prayer life. If you are new to dance as a sacred practice, I want to offer a few suggestions to help you take the first step.

PREPARING THE BODY

Picture a holy place, a place of pilgrimage, a temple, an alcove for an icon, or a memorial. It is easy to sense the care and profound respect in these places. Yet great spiritual teachers the world over propose that it is our own body, given over to prayer and God, that is the ultimate holy place. Those who dance to pray understand this more than most. The ground beneath our feet—the feeling of love rising in a posture, a pivot, an arch, or a run—helps us appreciate the dancer who said, "Dance is more than a form of movement; it is the altar upon which I offer myself."

When something is sacred to us, we return to it again and again, tend it, clear it of clutter, and infuse it with our intentions and prayers. What if we made time in our week to remember our body as a holy vessel and prepared it as an "altar" for dancing our devotion, intercession, and dreams?

When we smooth away our worries about "performing," we can begin to prepare body and soul as a meeting place for our conversations with the Holy. This will undoubtedly change some of our ideas about the role of self-care in our lives. The world is full of talk about self-care, but what if self-care is about more than diet, exercise, spas, and time-outs? What if the best self-care is soul-care? As Dr. Sheila Collins reminds us in her wonderful book *Stillpoint: The Dance of Selfcaring, Selfhealing,* "Dancing doesn't take energy, it makes energy! I didn't understand the reasons why dancing worked this way, but even my own children, when they were young, noticed the connection between dancing and my ability to cope. When they saw me losing patience with them, they would suggest, 'Don't you think it's time for you to take a dancing class, Mom?'"

For most of us, it's hard enough to take care of all that needs doing at home and at work, let alone create time for dancing. Seeing ourselves as a dancing altar is probably the last thing we'd imagine. A knotted heap or madhouse is a more apt metaphor for how we feel. Me, an altar? I am a ball of frenetic energy rolling over the countertop and computer desk of life, forgetting that *this* moment is an opportunity for gratitude and love. If I'm lucky, I hear my soul whisper, "Are you breathing? Are you dancing?" and take a deep breath. If I can stop and let my hand move from my heart to the heart of the Great Love, or bow before the Prime Mover, this crazy life transforms, and my dance with the Holy resumes.

How will you ready your body? How will you tend and keep it? How will you prepare?

Today, we spend vast sums on vacations to help us rejuvenate ourselves. Yet, until recently, the landscape of the Holy absorbed most of our resources. For thousands of years, humans put tremendous care into creating devotional objects related to dancing. Ceremony and prayer were the highest forms of entertainment. Trance-induced visions were the most prized form of travel. Artful preparations transformed each person's sacred dance accoutrements into gorgeous, holy devotion. I can imagine the stories, silence, songs, laughter, secrets, and contemplative moments that imbued all these preparations.

We're in a time when spiritual life is taking on greater importance. Whether or not our spirituality involves organized religion, even the small ways we prepare to dance with the Divine can nourish and transform us. We, too, can prepare through breath, music, space, clothing, imagery, a time to reflect—and, most important, to warm up body and soul.

BREATH

Movement begins with breath.

> Take a deep breath.
>
> Notice your chest slightly expand.
>
> Let your breath out with an audible sigh.
>
> As you exhale, welcome the release.
>
> Notice how your lungs move in rhythm.
>
> Experience your effortless breathing with gratitude.
>
> Each involuntary contraction and expansion is fundamental to human life.

I notice that I often hold my breath when I feel overextended or on edge. Or when I become withdrawn or hold back. As a person geared toward expressions of expansiveness, I am grateful that, through breath, my body graciously reminds me of the necessary balance between contraction and expansion. Even when I get too big for my britches or too shy to move, I can remind myself to take a deep breath and let it out with a sigh.

Breathing is so simple and yet, ultimately, it is one of the most profound and universal elements used in movement and prayer disciplines everywhere. In dancing, breath is elemental.

I invite you to take deep breaths and to sigh often. You can do this anywhere, anytime. Let your heart and soul move from your depths. Let breathing become a dance.

Breath Dance

~ Put on some calming music or seek out a quiet spot.

~ Settle yourself into a tranquil position.

~ Take a deep breath and let it out with a sigh. Do this several times.

~ Then widen your arms, to complement the "in and out" movement of your breath in any way that feels good to you.

~ Let your movement and breath quietly or enthusiastically contract and expand in sync.

~ Notice yourself being drawn to either your movement or your breath.

~ Let go of thinking about the "ins and outs" as your breath and movement interplay.

~ Let them evolve and go where they may. Sink into the moment.

~ To end, bring your arms together on your lap and spend a moment in thanks for the breath that gives you life and for movements that are part of the inspiration of breath.

❖ ❖ ❖

SPACE

Agathisos of Greece said, "Hail, space for the uncontained God." You are that space.

Widen your arms out into the air around you.

How much space do you "take up"?

How much space do you need?

Do you sense that your energy expands beyond your fingertips or feels close to your skin?

Some people need more space. Some need less. Julie Belafonte said of her famous dance mentor, Katherine Dunham, "'I think she projects about two feet of intense air around her." Personal space varies. For each of us, the space we require changes from day to day and season to season. Today you may need a big floor to move on; tomorrow you might need less.

Sacred space for dance is something we occupy. And it's something we can create. Our ancestors created sacred space with drums, fire, fabric, masks, dance, and song. Your dance space could be anywhere. It needn't be big or exclusively dedicated to dancing. I've danced in pews, cars, and hallways. In many a sanctuary I've adapted my movement to a patch of space in front of the altar. I've incorporated marble steps, immovable pulpits, pianos, organs, and choir stalls.

Open space is wonderful but not crucial. The space within you is what matters most. This means it is quite possible to dance even in a prison cell, in your bathroom, or in your backyard. Or you could find a spot under a great tree. Natural surroundings are perfect places to dance, but so is your living room. Push back a few chairs and create a space. Wherever you can let the spirit move is a good place to dance.

Randall and Sharon, a couple in their sixties, warm up and share movement several times each week in their small condominium living room. One moves or tells a story while the other witnesses. They've learned to trust their body wisdom in their spiritual life as individuals and as a couple. Sometimes a single companion is all you need to create holy space. Between you and him, the subtle, blessed territory of sacred space opens up.

On the other hand, the kind of physical space we have inspires the way we move. When I walk into a school cafeteria with racks of tables and a tired linoleum floor, I hesitate to move, lie down, jump, or fall. Concrete floors are notoriously poor shock absorbers. Even the youngest folks suffer injuries on nonforgiving floors. A wooden or cushioned floor is kinder to human joints.

Those who enter our InterPlay studio are struck by the massive floor-to-ceiling concrete support forms and exposed brick walls. Light filters through large windows and bounces off glowing pine floorboards. Chairs, floor seats, and blankets are all available. Shelving for shoes near the entry suggests, "Take off your shoes, you're entering holy ground." All who come through the door see that movement happens in this place. They sense that the body is welcome. Even those who are timid are enticed, and children immediately sense a freedom to run and slide across the floor.

Making space for breath and movement is a powerful affirmation of life. Whether the ground you find yourself on is earthen, tile, carpet, or parquet, giving yourself space to dance is what is key.

In *Wisdom Comes Dancing: Selected Writing of Ruth St. Denis on Dance, Spirituality and the Body*, a wonderful line from Ruth St. Denis, the grandmother of sacred dance, encourages us to open this space within. She instructs us to "begin from the center with the purification of the first environment, our own garment of flesh, and by the conception of our bodies. From there we radiate outward into the surrounding world." In other words, as much as you might want a "perfect" spot in which to dance, it is really the other way around: You make the space around you holy when you dance.

DRESS

Dancing isn't about costuming. For the most part, special clothes or shoes aren't necessary. In the classic musical film *Singin' in the Rain*, Gene Kelly performed one of film's most memorable dances in a wet raincoat. Whatever you wear is fine. I think of the many institutions where I have taught the wisdom of the body and the role of movement to "people of the chairs" wearing hosiery, heels, and tight-fitting suits. Are they comfortable? I don't know. But I do know they can move.

Obviously, what you wear does affect your range of motion and does influence your desire to move. Do your clothes invite

you to dance? I once donned a medieval a
weight of the garment, the deep pockets bene
ing my hands, and the heavy veil restricting
posture like the nuns seen in old movies. Pai
way the outfit intensified my body's verticality, but my movements were minimal.

When you dress for sacred movement, imagine clothing that invites you to dance. I once saw glorious photos of African children who adorned themselves in nature's bounty, making their bodies into remarkable altars of beauty. As I look around the world at sacred dancers, I see garments of gladness, flashing with mirrors, feathers, and every hue of the rainbow. They manifest the dream world, reflect back the spirits of trees, creatures, and exuberant exaggerations of our human auras and energies. In India I grow jealous of the flow and richly saturated colors of women's clothing. Even in a slum, women look stunning. No wonder Indian women move with such ease and grace. Drapes of fabric, wreathing bodices wrapped in saris, make each woman into a minor goddess.

You might want to experiment with flowing loose skirts, pants, dresses, or shirts. Sweatpants, too, are fine. Put them on and try them out to see if this encourages your dancing. Or perhaps you need to pare down to move. Removing layers is a powerful metaphor for spiritual life. Taking off shoes and coats, letting skin breathe and limbs move without constriction is an invitation to freedom. Workout clothes are made for this purpose. Or, if the attire of ballet, tap, and modern dance inspires you, you might enjoy wearing tights and leotards.

As for me, I like dancing in street clothes. I've come to hate having to make a big deal out of changing my clothes every time I enter or leave the studio. Besides, I want to feel the freedom to dance anywhere, whether I do or not. I like to imagine dancing down the aisles of grocery stores or up flights of stairs at the library (even though I usually don't). Dancing in ordinary clothes rks as long as they don't bind my legs or arms. It helps that I wear pants that stretch and long shirts that move with me. The only concession I make is donning special dancers' tennis shoes to support my aging feet. For me, the line between dancing to dance, dancing to live, and dancing to pray is enjoyably blurry.

How do you want to clothe your dancing? Why not wrap yourself in beauty, in comet tails and sunrises, beneath a coat of many colors, or in a skin shiny with sweat? When you let dance dress you, she makes you her beloved. Barefooted or with a decorated walker, any attention to what you wear can enhance your movement.

MUSIC

Music is dance's somatic twin. Get a rhythm going, and dance follows. The two hate being separated. In many ways music is a sanctuary, and dancers are its priests. Music creates landscape, and dance travels through it, directing the energy.

A *National Geographic* magazine pictured three Hawaiian women dancing in a living room. A ukulele case sat on an ice cooler. The accompanying article described the scene: "When Hawaiian studies teachers Linda Pacheco and Harriet Daog broke out ukuleles, their friend and colleague Sabra Kauka said, 'I couldn't resist, so I got up and started to dance.' That's one side of hula, the spontaneous display of joy. But there's another, more measured form reserved for special occasions, reverence for *kupuna* (honored elders and ancestors) and reverence for the past. Together, hula's music and dance form the sacred center of Hawaiian culture."

While you might not play a ukulele, you probably have a CD player, an iPod, or other means of playing music. You can use your voice, breath, hand and foot rhythms, or the sounds of the world around you to accompany your dancing.

If possible, I suggest that you gather a few CDs—at least one that is nonrhythmic and soothing, one that is upbeat and energizing, and one that blends instrumental melodies and rhythm. While you may love music that has a heavy beat or songs with powerful lyrics, these types of music tend to restrict freedom in movement. Words and rhythms act like outside authorities. Even "spiritual" songs, like "Amazing Grace," can dictate your emotion. Sometimes this is desirable, creating exactly the effect you want. But, for ongoing practice, I recommend finding music that provides room for the myriad of unspoken images and sensations of any given season or mood.

The challenge is to wear all music like a loose garment. If the beat is insistent, you can still hold still. If women's voices fill the air with assurance, you can still stomp and plead. Doris Humphrey said in *The Art of Making Dances*, "Don't be a slave to the music." Good advice, for whatever type of music you choose for dancing your prayers.

Live music is the best companionship of all. If everyone had an Amar Khalsa, we'd all be in dancing heaven. I met Amar decades ago when he first sat down to play keyboard at a rehearsal. Phil and I immediately wanted to invite him into our company. As a meditative American Sikh with roots in Methodist Church choirs, Amar's forte is play. Devotion is his organizing principle. He both holds and releases dance with his music making as he willingly provides the beginnings and ends of pieces. More amazing, though, is his ability to perform on multiple instruments—keyboard or flute, harmonium or guitar—either improvising or playing compositions. Ready to make music for every moment, he'll support someone who wants to sing an improvised prayer. He has very little ego in his music; blessing others seems to be his mission. If we had sainthood or knighthood for musicians, I would nominate Amar.

Although there are few Amars, music for the soul needn't be perfect. Our own ability to move in time with whatever is going on is how we generate magic. Start the music. Enjoy it. It doesn't need to be "sacred music" to create a sacred dance. A kinesthetic relationship with the Divine is not bound to prescribed reper-toires of religious sounds. Hip-hop, R&B, classical, pop, world, reggae, oldies, and new compositions are all potential accompa-niment. Music and dance relate to every aspect of life. Why not aspire to be like the Hawaiians, whose traditional music evokes spontaneous, joyful dance as well as a means of attuning to their most reverential reflexes?

IMAGES

There are places on earth where images of divine dancers are everywhere. In India, Shiva dances on dashboards and in street shrines. A sculpture of St. Francis in Bangalore shows him with his robes flying and his arms outspread. In Malawi, painted rows of figures—arms lifted, one foot up, the other flexed into the earth, everyone dancing to the beat of the drum—say everything about the spirit of this African culture and belief system.

Imagery can inspire our dancing practice and remind us that dance is essential to our lives. What images support your dancing aspirations? A sculpture, a poster, old ballet shoes, a beautiful card, or the lively flame of a simple candle? Hanging on the wall of my living room is an Australian print of an aboriginal figure dancing a transformation from large bird to human, as well as a Haitian mermaid, arms extended in blessing. Parading over my sliding-glass door is a six-foot painted strip of Malawian dancers and drummers. Small paintings of flamenco, Thai, and indige-nous Warli dancers carry on the theme throughout the room. Movement is how I celebrate and see the world.

Your own small or large art projects can visually encourage your dancing. Do you doodle? Why not let your hand "dance" on the page? The free movement of a hand dancing color onto a page in one continuous line can say a lot. In her book *Praying with Color,* dancer Sybil MacBeth describes doodling as her form of prayer and recommends trying it. Let your hand dance with col-ored pens or pencils and some smooth white paper.

Do you make collages? Try using dance as the subject. Juxtapose any theme with the notion of dancing and see what images come to mind when you relate things like dance and family, dance and peace, dance and trees. Once you get going, you'll see more and more dancing connections.

Or you might simply light a candle. The movement of a flame can remind you that there is a fire inside, alive and always flickering. A wind chime activated by a breeze or trembling leaves just outside a window are worthy testaments to the spirit of movement.

The one thing I'd caution you on is not to get stuck idealizing dance. A beautiful image might keep you at arm's length, telling you that you'll never be like that, or cake your consciousness in overly romantic notions of "dancerly otherness." Worst of all, you may flatten dance's dynamism into two-dimensional, static symbols, set apart from you.

I'll never forget visiting a man who had a beautiful painting of dancers on his living room wall. Unfortunately, his heart didn't match his art. He was critical of me for dancing in church. "Who ordained you?" he blurted out. I answered, "Your church." My dancing was a distraction and an insult to his religious sensibilities. I don't think he'd ever had a chance to dance himself.

Dance is not meant to freeze into an image, but an image can free up a dance. Look around your home. What image inspires dance? Give it a place of honor. Hold it. Touch it. Let it move you. Making dance part of the way you see the world can open your eyes to the beauty of motion all around you.

THOUGHTFUL REFLECTIONS

Dance stirs consciousness. Who knows what will break through to the surface into awareness, voices, memories, or poems? For those who open to the reverie that exists just beyond the limits of analytical, critical thinking, endless streams of revelation await. But dance is such a transient reality that, without a witness, an audience, or a place to reflect, these thoughts and feelings can easily vanish.

I encourage you to keep a dancing journal. There is nothing like becoming your own researcher of body wisdom. Write down bits and pieces of body data to honor the physicality of a moment or reflect on larger sweeps of awareness. Write down intentions and dreams about dancing. You make your dancing sacred by taking time to reflect on your feelings, memories, or insights and become your own witness.

Thirty seconds of writing might be enough. Free-associate. Have a "correspondence" between you and your body, you and your soul, you and whatever or whoever appears in your mind while you dance. Even if all you do is draw rough images or write down a few lines, the link between your body wisdom and your thoughts will grow stronger, similar to the practice of writing down dreams. (Some people, in fact, consider dance to be a dream-body.)

For me, the poetry that arises from word fragments and images is the easiest form of writing. Because it does not have to make perfect sense, I can record a sensory moment in a few lines that hang together on memory's page. This is what I mean by reflecting.

Many people resist connecting dance with words. I understand. Dancing resists definition. Words may seem to take away the sense of mystery. Yet the stories, dreams, and thoughts that come to light in the process of moving are a way to claim the incredible gifts of the dancing soul. In our culture we value and use language, so if we fail to honor dancing with written and spoken words, the powerful help and healing that dance offers may remain hidden to our world and even to ourselves. Words crystallize dance's unique experience in our consciousness.

Other ways to reflect include collecting, as I do, words of encouragement from other dancers. Their memoirs, poetry, and articulations are inspiring. Reading Ruth St. Denis's memoir, *An Unfinished Life*, and writing my own memoir, *Chasing the Dance of Life: A Faith Journey*, have been two of the most important theological and spiritual platforms of my spiritual practice. Though it's almost impossible for me to write directly about dancing (much like the difficulty of adequately describing encounters with God), the way dance shapes me, teaches me, and rewards me with love and compassion is undeniable. I can see that clearly when I put it in writing.

Reflections can also take the form of conversation. You may find that talking with a friend, a minister, or a spiritual director every now and then helps you reflect on your movement experience. Betsey Beckman, a dance therapist and spiritual director in Washington state, believes that creative experiences like dance can open "a fountain of expression" for emotions and longings that most of us don't easily put into words, and that the more we dance, the more our words may grow wings, longing to move through the world and be shared. We are fortunate today that more and more spiritual leaders are acquainted with the power of movement as a spiritual practice. Any person who shares your sense of discovering dance as a spiritual medium can be a good companion. Later in this book, I'll talk about ways of being a "sacred witness" to each other's dance.

Reflections are like a second breath, the deep inhale after a first encounter. If you take time to reflect, you ground your body wisdom in your own truth. Those who go into religious training and development have similar practices, although they may not be as present, personal, and physically rooted. If you choose to reflect on your dancing, I assure you that you will grow in noticeable ways.

WARMING UP BODY AND SOUL

Preparation is good, but nothing replaces the act of actually beginning to move. Warming up is perhaps the most important provision for dance in any practice. As you take this step, know that there is no right way. This bears repeating. *There is no right way.* There is only you and the dance of life, the Great Dance from which we came and to which we return. Releasing your worry or concern about moving in the right way will make it easier to feel a sacred connection to heaven and earth.

Most of us need a few minutes to enter our bodies, to become attuned to our sensations and breath, and to let our muscles soften from their holding patterns into more pliable flexibility. I often hear people say after just ten minutes of the following easygoing warm-up, "I feel more present, more relaxed, lighter." Their comments, and my own direct experience, constantly remind me that every day we sacrifice our bodies to the exploits of the mind and work. We are stiff and breathless, and our focus narrows to the point of excluding the world around us. *In our head* is an understatement. Many of us forget that there are enjoyable, relaxed sensations to be had just a few movements away. Not until a major life transition, an illness, or an injury occurs do we stop taking these sensations for granted.

I used to hate warming up. "Just let me dance," I thought. I was fortunate that my body had the stamina and strength to go for it. As I age, of course, that is not the case. Happily, my current warm-up has become as much my prayer as any other part of dancing.

Warming up can occur just by seeing things you already do with the intent of dance. With music or in silence, you could just begin to walk. Your steps could be random or purposeful. Let go of worrying about getting anywhere. As you step, or roll in a wheelchair, observe one movement flowing into the next; inertia will become a thing of the past. Momentum is your friend. Don't discount these basic steps. The dance of life is not concerned with frills. Joy dances on this earth one step at a time.

Your body knows what it needs.

Start by squirming around.
Squirm your bones and blood and breath.
As you squirm, notice what places are tight or loose, flexible or stiff.
Stretch and squirm these places.

Unless you plan on dancing vigorously, simple stretching and remobilizing your various bodily systems are sufficient.

Every Friday morning, I, along with a dozen movers, enter a space where the wood floor and high ceiling offer warmth and openness. The large concrete sections stabilizing the brick walls always remind me of pillars in a cathedral or large trees that appear to hold up the sky. This is my sanctuary. I touch a button on a boom box and a rich musical landscape fills the room. We remove our shoes and begin.

I invite you to "join us" in these steps of our warm-up.

Warm-Up for Body and Soul

~ Take a deep breath and let out a sigh.

~ Shake out one hand and then another. Shake out your legs and your bottom and whatever you've metaphorically been "sitting on." Shake out your voice. Shake your body down into the earth like salt and pepper. Let your feet, ankles, and legs help you feel the ground.

~ Reach your arms overhead and then out wide to the sides. (You might want to think of the tree of life while you're doing this.) Wrap your arms around your trunk and embrace the solidity of your body for a moment.

~ Slowly drop over, bowing to the earth. (Take care of your own limitations as you hang down.) Nod yes and no to let gravity help your neck let go of the effort of holding up your head. Then, taking care of your back, roll up your spine, coming back up to standing in the best way for you. Repeat this sequence a few times.

~ Open your chest like one of those mastheads on the prow of a ship, and then contract back into your spine. Sense your spirit move to the front of your body and curl back in as you repeat this.

~ With your feet planted, twist from side to side, letting your open arms swing and provide momentum.

~ Gradually squirm and move down into your hips. Do a little "fake hula," circling your hips, welcoming the deeper and sometimes less familiar movements of your lower body. Groaning is welcome.

~ Massage your feet into the floor like a cat kneading a favorite object. Let your feet take you to a different place in the room.

~ When you stop, swing one leg forward and back and notice the ease or challenge of holding your balance. Try the other leg.

~ Take a deep breath. Open your mouth and eyes wide open, and then scrunch them closed a few times. Give your face a little massage.

~ (You could end here or continue by warming up with the following four dynamics of swing, thrust, shape, and hang.)

~ Swing your arms from side to side. Let the sweeping and rocking motions soothe and energize you.

~ Move into flinging and thrusting your arms and legs for a few moments to gather and direct energy.

~ When you are ready, take a still shape. Let the shape transition to another one. Enjoy the possibilities of stretching into each shape, experiencing the movement and the rest in each position.

~ Sculptural gestures may emerge. Hold still in them as long as you like. Some may feel like prayer.

~ Finally, in hang mode, as if letting your weight and muscles hang loose, try some slow, smooth movements, what I call "fake t'ai chi." Following the flow of your body, listen to your impulses and desires. Your movements can be like a river, energetically and spatially taking you wherever they want to go.

~ You may be surprised that there is more or less energy available than you imagined. As your warm-up deepens into meditation, moving into stillness or lying down is perfectly acceptable. Let this time of movement meditation continue for as long as you like.

~ When you are ready, you might take a deep breath and offer a sustained vocal tone. It is fine to move or to be still as you vocalize.

~ Make soft or loud sounds to shift your voice from one tone to another. Vocalizing opens your chest, liberates your breath, and warms you up from the inside out in a kind of wordless prayer.

❖ ❖ ❖

On those Friday mornings when we come to the end of our warm-up, I hear the voices of people in the room wander, merge, and play. The sound is plaintive, gorgeous, intense, or quirky, according to the day. Our improvised singing ends on its own, leaving us in a stillness that no one wants to break. The quiet feels palpable—perhaps, the real reason we come. Peace and serenity are ours. Afterwards, we gather to notice and reflect. Gratitude is always present.

Whatever happens for you, remember, the most important thing is to listen to what your bodyspirit wants and find a way to heed your hunger. Trusting your body to pray is one of the greatest gifts you can give yourself.

You do not need to draw definitive lines between preparation, warming up, and actual dancing. Think of a flower before it is even a bud. It gradually takes form and, when the time is right, opens to the sun to then unfold and eventually achieve a full bloom. Entering dance is like that. Each movement leads to the next. Creaky bones moisten into languid expressions. Small breaths get deeper. One woman with painful arthritis said, "I didn't hurt at all when we were moving!"

If none of this gets you out of your chair, and you need some-one to say it, I will. "Get up. It's time to move body and soul. Take a deep breath and let it out with a sigh. Let the dance begin."

CHAPTER THREE

UNLOCKING THE DANCE OF JOY

"On with dance, let joy be unconfined, is my motto; whether there's any dance to dance or any joy to be unconfined."

—*Mark Twain*

Joyride ... "Joy to the World" ... joystick ... jump for joy. Joy and action go hand in hand. Dietrich Bonhoeffer once said, "If you do a good job for others, you heal yourself at the same time, because a dose of joy is a spiritual cure."

Joy is pure gold, a source that prompts our dance as much as it is dancing's outcome. Whether joy feels like daily bread—the "Eureka, I found it" vein running through life—or something over the rainbow, it is the work of spiritual practice to call it forth.

In the sitcom *Perfect Strangers,* the character Balki, a naive immigrant from a Greek isle, would say to his cousin/roommate Larry, "Now we are so happy, we do the dance of joy!" Larry, in spite of being Americanized, learned to spring up off the couch and face Balki as they grabbed each other's waists or shoulders and sang, "Di, Di, Di, Di, Di, Di." In less than a minute, they vigorously kicked out their legs from side to side, alternately jumped in the air, and bobbed their heads in a pecking motion, singing, "Hey, hey, hey, hey!" For the finale, one jumped into the other's arms with a rousing "Ha!"

Somehow I can imagine Jesus better when I think of Balki. When Jesus said, "These things I have spoken to you, that my joy may be in you, and that your joy may be full (John 15:11), I think he was telling us to cultivate an aliveness that may not even make sense in our circumstances. The emotions of hate, anger, and fear have trouble coexisting with happiness. And did you know that the word for *rejoice* in Aramaic, Jesus's native tongue, means "to dance"?

Dancing is joy's signature. To dance with joy depends on three master keys that unlock the gifts of embodiment: the grace key, the maker key, and the fun-lover key. You may already have these keys or you may need to get them out and practice using them a bit. Either way, to unlock the doors of body and soul, you'll need to take them in hand.

THE GRACE KEY

You know what stress feels like—tight, constricted, cranky, sleepless, hyped-up. Now think of the opposite sensations. Was there a time recently that you were really enjoying yourself or feeling relaxed? You can feel that in your body, too. In my InterPlay work we call these physical sensations the "physicality of grace." Breathing, spacious, energized, awake, openhearted, laughing, silly—the spectrum of grace in our bodily experience is wide and generous.

You know the things that tend to create these sensations, too: hiking in nature, swimming, knitting, making love, singing, family time, reading a good book, dancing, eating delicious food. Certain friends and animals can be counted on to increase our grace factor. If we want more "grace" experiences, we can choose to have them.

In my book *What the Body Wants,* I wrote that I was taught in church that "grace is a gift, undeserved." I was to feel "unworthy of grace" and yet expectant. Grace seemed like a giant lottery game to me. What a gamble: Buy the right ticket, go to the right vendor, and God's magic lands in your lap—maybe.

I like the dictionary's definition of *grace* better. Coming from the Latin *gratia*, it means "favor, esteem, kindness, pleasing, and agreeable." It has to do with thanksgiving, expressions of gratitude before meals, physical ease and beauty, hospitality, and divine blessing. Poets say that animals and trees can have it. The theological definition comes something like fourteenth in the dictionary list. What I love best of all is that dancing generates social grace. That's why parents still send kids to dance class. It helps keep them from clobbering each other and absentmindedly running into walls.

The physicality of grace is neither masculine nor feminine. Athletes on a basketball court convince me of this. I watch their fluid motion as it is followed to its conclusion, the pressure of two feet kissing the floor, the push, the muscles springing into a leap, the arch that carries a ball from the center of the body up through the shooting arms, releasing it in a splendid, confident delivery. Millions of us gather to witness this elegant, efficient, purposeful, *graceful* movement. The fact that it is part of a game, released from real necessities, fills it with the whimsy and beauty of the sacred. The player has a gift to give; we are the recipients.

You won't see me on a court leaping in the air, but my body, too, knows how to extend and flow. So does yours. What brings you grace? Notice your body when you are in the midst of graceful actions, like rowing, skiing, swing dancing, swinging a child, or simply swaying. I've been paying more attention lately to what I enjoy. In a Pilates class, I am more alert to sensations inside my core. I can feel the tensile pressure as a slight tightening that gives me a surge of physical engagement. In dance classes, they sometimes call this "pulling up." I used to try so hard to suck in my gut, mistaking a flat stomach for this deeper feeling of connection. I relish the renewal of this bodily experience even more as I am aware of having lost touch with it. The dancerly power in my body sings, "I'm back!"

I've noticed, too, how much I enjoy the feel of a simple pivot on the ball of my foot. Turning, I rotate into a brief spiral of motion, and my attention whirls around with me. Entering a new way of being in those moments, I am reminded that the word *repent* means "to turn around." Changing my point of view, experiencing the freedom to see the world differently, refreshes me. Sometimes I spin and spin like a whirling dervish, amazed at my ability to stay upright and watch the world around me melt into a soft blur.

Watching others expressing themselves in their favorite ways stimulates yet more grace. Gliding, tracing serpentine paths, hopping, casting out unseen forces, flying, dropping, hunching down, tightening into a ball, prostrating for minutes upon minutes—a body absorbed in moving *is* grace.

When we take hold of the physicality of the "grace key" to benefit our own bodies and support the grace in other bodies, we begin to unlock the treasure chest of the sublime.

Dance to Savor Grace

~ Begin by moving one of your arms. Notice its natural coordination as it reaches out and extends.

~ Add your other arm. Notice the way your two arms immediately engage each other, perfect partners in a single act.

~ Imagine lifting, embracing, and dancing in gratitude as you remember an experience that brings you ordinary grace, like the smile of a passerby, a waitress's accent, a child's laughter.

~ Breathing, touching these memories, dance and savor the beauty your body knows.

~ In union with these sensations, conclude and give thanks.

❖ ❖ ❖

THE MAKER KEY

Humans make things. I look around my office at all the stuff we've compiled, sorted, and assembled and see row upon row of glowing glass paperweights, artwork on the walls, and crazy pictures of people grouped in dozens of positions, raising their arms in a big *wheeee* for the camera. And that's just on the surface. It doesn't include the stuff we've made downstairs in the studio or out in the world.

Making is a primary act. We make time, make dinner, make love, make a date, make a face, make the bed, make friends, make a joke, make babies, make sure, make way, make amends, make space, make over, make believe, make up, make waves, make a deal, make a getaway, make a promise.

Are we creative or what? We may follow recipes and rules, downplaying our ingenuity, but the urge to fashion the world is in us all, from the people driving tractors to clerks neatly stocking the shelves at the store. Creativity is not so much a feeling as it is the everyday reinvention of our relationship with the material of life.

Those who use the art of dancing as an entry to spiritual practice hold the "maker key." On a basic level, this key unlocks our motions. On another level, it unlocks our ability to make a world. This may seem like a strange thing to say, but between a dance's beginning and end, we do form a little world. This creative universe doesn't require a big bang. Simply initiating, getting a movement going, following it through, and coming to a stop—that is all that is needed. What happens in between inevitably takes on a life of its own. Sometimes, this little dancing world has the power to make us, too. Remarkably, our making is a collaboration with Spirit and life.

To make something, we must employ a kind of imagination that rests as much in our muscles as it does in our minds. "Kinesthetic imagination" leads us into dreamlike, emotive, and symbolic forms of intelligence that take on a narrative quality similar to the way we might understand a musician's score. We use our imagination in both producing and "perceiving" a dance.

Consider a dog sleeping and dreaming. His nervous system doesn't know the difference between the rabbit he chases in his mind as he sleeps on the sofa, and the real creature he chased earlier that day. Both rouse his kinesthetic sense of tension and anticipation. Or think of how you feel after a nightmare. Are you tense? Even though nothing bad actually happened, you feel the effects of what you are *imagining* in your body. Or when you are commandeered by thought-ghosts, you may tense, jitter, and balk. Or if you are considering worst-case scenarios, you may pace, agitate, and sweat.

Certainly, kinesthetic imagination may also engender kinder imagined realities. How might images of animals, plants, ancestors, words, angels, heroes, higher powers, and gods affect not only our present-time bodies but also our spiritual life? A play, a dance, or a skit—even though they are virtual, made-up worlds—can improve the way we think and feel.

Our kinesthetic imagination serves as a mighty portal for reaching beyond ordinary sensibilities. Observe the ability of children to transform their world into a parallel reality. This charms us. The five-year-old does not think, "Let me pretend that I'm a cat." She gives herself to catness. Similarly, when indigenous people put on the costumes of bear and tiger and bird, they aren't pretending to be these animals. They *become* them. The dancers' movements take on the essence of the animal as much as possible, enabling them to view the world from the point of view and wisdom of the creatures that inhabit them.

This kind of kinesthetic imagination is something to preserve in each other, not abandon. To be able to play between the real and "made-up" worlds is to function on the highest level. It takes sophistication to relate to multiple realities. Those who cultivate this practice can use their ability to dance new worlds into being. This is of great benefit.

In an *AARP* magazine story, I was fascinated to learn about former professional dancer Cynthia Toussaint. She had developed a complex regional pain syndrome that went undiagnosed for fifteen years. Bedridden in a fetal position and unable to care for herself, she finally found doctors who allowed her to try movement therapy, deep relaxation techniques, and guided imagery. In bedside sessions, Touissant's therapist assisted her as she "conjured up make-believe ballet classes," where, with the therapist's help, she constructed whole sequences of dancing that she did entirely in her mind. "Taking dance class" three times a week began to heal her. Her muscles began letting go. In a month she began to sit up, walk, and shower with assistance. Her kinesthetic imagination made it possible for her to receive the physical therapy that further reduced her pain.

To "make believe" is also what people of faith must do. Since we can't literally see the Divine, we must meet Mystery with our God-given imaginations. I believe that when we dance, the body contacts the Prime Mover through our original languages— movement and sound. The result is a beautiful prayer, like the one composed by the psalmist who said, "O Lord, you have searched me and known me! Thou knowest when I sit down and when I rise up; Thou discernest my thoughts from afar ... even before a word is on my tongue, lo, O Lord, thou knowest it altogether" (Psalm 139:1, 2, 4).

I spoke with a man who takes a movement class. Arriving at the studio after work, he changed into some sweatpants and joined the warm-up. It had been a long day, and he wasn't that "into" it, something he struggles with a lot. As usual, he caught himself looking at the clock. Only ten minutes had passed. Why was he so bored? Knowing his tendency to observe rather than participate in life, he took a deep breath and chose to enter into the dance. He felt himself viscerally "drop down" and let himself experience the creative process. The next thing he knew, the class was over. He'd gone places, seen things, and thoroughly enjoyed himself. Later, he told me, "I guess I wasn't enjoying it before because I was in my head."

It makes a difference if we observe or participate in life. To "make a difference" is high on the list of human priorities and a key to spiritual activism. When we become makers, we leave behind victimization and claim the power that we have, the ability to do something humble, simple, and productive that creates a better, more beautiful world. If each one of us took up our "maker key," the dance of life might look less like something to react to and more enticing. I believe we'd have more of Bonhoeffer's "dose of joy."

If you want more connection with mystery, intuition, and surprise, it is your wandering, dreaming soul that may know best how to arrive at its destination. Dance is perfectly suited to opening the door of conscious, symbolic connection. Make a dance and you'll make a difference in the very ground of your being. Plant your feet on a little spot of earth and imagine what you want to contribute on your spiritual path.

Dancing a Spiritual Journey

~ Play some uplifting music. A drumbeat can be helpful.

~ Notice where your feet are. Stand, if you are able, and take a deep breath.

~ With your eyes closed or open, very slowly let your feet move in any direction, as if you were making a path.

~ Notice any feelings or thoughts about your path. Are you moving toward or away from something?

~ Play with stopping, starting, and changing directions.

~ Include the play of your arms, legs, and torso.

~ As you move, you may begin to "see" and "know" things that hadn't occurred to you before. Take note of them for later reflection.

~ As your dance concludes, come back to stillness.

~ Look down at your feet and honor the imagination that led you on this brief journey, bringing you insight and guidance beyond your normal sight.

❖ ❖ ❖

THE FUN-LOVER KEY

One of the great pleasures—and powers—of movement is that it's *fun*. This is immediately obvious in the joy of sports teams, theater ensembles, parades, and billions of fans.

Dancing for fun snuck up on Reverend Barbara Nixon:

I am back from Mexico where I cannot claim to have done anything, really, except pray and rest. This combo included walks on the beach, a bit of reading, much music, food (especially fresh coconut and hand-patted corn tortillas), sunset and sunrise viewing, and, oh my, dancing in the dark on the beach every night. Silly me, who thinks I have no partner—I danced with waves and the moon and the sand. It was a joy. I fell into the sky— true periwinkle—day after day and sometimes didn't come back for hours. I noticed yet again for the first time, and always, that life is constant motion. The only way to have it at all is to show up in the moment.

When I dance, everyone tells me, "You certainly looked like you were having fun." Enjoyment is tonic enough. Fun is rapturous, like the conga line that boogies every year through San Francisco's financial district on Dance Everywhere Day. Wanting to participate and feeling slightly rambunctious, a group of us went outside, put a drummer at each of the four corners of 23rd and Telegraph Avenue, and began drumming, while the rest of us waved banners and made merry to the beat. Soyinka stole the show, dancing right in the middle of the street.

Although there weren't many cars, the danger added spice to joy, making it fun, fun, fun. As we passed out peacock feathers, other fun-lovers couldn't help but hitch themselves to such a dance.

Too often we think that spiritual discipline involves suffering: "Unless I suffer, I am not learning or growing." But if we are seeking joy, does it make sense to get there through pain? Movement as a sacred practice calls for an ethic of play where fun as a spiritual principle takes priority, even if it undermines the calcified, puritanical assumptions of the past with such "radical" ideas as:

~ I don't have to be articulate
~ I have all the time in the world
~ Everything belongs
~ All creations are welcome
~ Curiosity rules
~ I can surprise and be surprised
~ I decide how I want to play
~ I decide when to rest

Sound too good to be true? Sound insane? Think of fun this way: Playfulness is not the opposite of work; it's just a terrific way to get work done. Fun keeps imagination greased and spirit at the ready. It balances out egocentric ambition and elevates the most mundane acts to the heights of holy amusement. The one rule is that if you want to poke fun at someone, it's best to poke fun at yourself. Fun at the expense of others may shine light on truth, but it can just as easily wound.

The "fun-lover key" has cool grooves and notches on it, embellished with words like *sexy, savoring, challenging, witty, wonder-full*—even *daring*. The idea that fun is not safe is noteworthy. Many of us want to domesticate spirituality, each other, and God. But when we try to create a "nice" God, we deprive ourselves of the open-ended, mysterious, gut and groin power of sacred relationship. In the East they call this the "root chakra." It's where the fire comes from.

Spirituality is meant to challenge. There are many initiations to go through. Learning to dance with God, to allow spontaneous, synchronous connection can be one of them. Dancing is mystical play; it's "festival."

Stan Stuart makes his living working with computer software, a profession that is somehow symbiotic with those who dance. His paychecks give him the freedom to play, while his degrees in music and ministry feed his passion for creating, nurturing, and finding meaning in life. He dances on the floor, at the keyboard, and in his heart, as the lines of his poem "Festival Inside" reveal:

I have a festival going on inside me.
Outside may be turbulent or mundane,
Ratcheted or insane.
Inside is celebratory.
Like a laboratory.
With a new discovery of my recovery.

Those who have fun both fully enter themselves and get over themselves at the same time. One way to do this is through a "dance of release."

Dance of Release

~ Place your fingertips in the groove between your eyes, in the spot where your insistent worries and your attempts to figure things out collect.
~ Playfully fling this focused energy up in the air with a wheeee.
~ Try it a few more times. Let this little physical reminder help you playfully release what holds you back, and open your mind and body.

~ Are there other places that are holding you back?
Play with flinging out some *wheeee* motions from
these areas, too.

~ If this is fun, make a dance out of it. *Wheeee,
wheeee, wheeee* all the way home to a looser you.

❖ ❖ ❖

Fun comes easier with company. Is there someone who inspires you to laugh and go a little crazy? Sharon does that for me. She literally performs casts of characters that liberate me to take on a persona of my own, like "Tree," "Fairy Godmother," and "Spiral Lena." What a relief to be a character, one who is not so serious!

Matt had no trouble finding friends to dance "crazy" with him. A popular 2008 YouTube clip shows this big white guy dancing with people all over the planet. His movement is bouncy and happy, and others exuberantly join in, from Mumbai to Montreal, Singapore to Soweto, Tel Aviv to Timbuktu. All of them look like they are enjoying doing the "Matt Dance." One of those who danced with him wrote on her blog, "It brought me to happy tears because it is pure joy, no politics, no attachments, no stress, no problems, just people having fun together doing the same thing (dancing badly) at the same time, all over our big beautiful world." If Matt's fun-loving movements connected a world of people, why can't ours? It is fun to find each other as a walking, stumbling, jumping, running, dancing human family.

Perhaps one of the best ways to unlock playfulness is to invite your trickster out to play, the part of you that's a mischievous imp. I'm talking about that powerhouse of energy, information, truth, and silliness hiding behind your reserve, the part of you that wants to say what's not being said or is eager to introduce the opposite side of things. This trickster can be totally annoying and magnificently comedic.

You may not know that you can create a chortle. One friend revealed a trick she plays on herself while cooking. She talks out loud in a high-pitched "Julia Child" voice, describing every ingredient and step in her dinner preparations. When she told me this, it made me laugh because she is shy, sensitive, and petite—the very opposite of Julia Child.

Surprising antics can produce some wonderful physical comedy or at least shift your mood. Give these playful trickster dances a try. Give each one ten seconds. That should do it.

Trickster Dances

~ Thrust your pelvis forward and walk around the room. Can you keep a straight face?

~ Exaggerate any body part or movement. This works especially well if you make fun of your own movement style.

~ Try holding your thighs together or walking while keeping your feet far apart from each other. Unexpected actions are often funny.

~ Hold your face in a strange position and keep it there. Let your moves flow from your facial expression.

~ Dance in a completely jerky, quirky way to "Amazing Grace."

❖ ❖ ❖

Nothing helps distance us from life's seriousness like fun. I know a Presbyterian minister who hates the song "Amazing Grace." Playing with it redeemed it for her.

An Episcopalian friend who is a slightly overweight expert in Robert's Rules of Order frequently shows up as "Zelda," a teller of prophetic lies. She dances into the room with at least one feather boa, eyes the attractive men, and exclaims, "Everyone loves Zelda!"

At a national women's meeting of spiritual leaders, it happened that we met on the dawning of Aquarius Day, foretold by astrologists and celebrated in the musical *Hair.* Everyone stood up in high amusement, arms lifted, swaying in Woodstockian bliss to collectively belt out, "When the moon is in the seventh house and Jupiter aligns with Mars...." We got out the whole chorus as if we were in the sixties. Song, dance, joy, and high humor brought us together in a silly, but sublimely memorable and embodied way.

Unlocking joy is dance's mission. Mother Teresa once said, "Joy is a net of love by which you can catch souls. A joyful heart is the inevitable result of a heart burning with love." Rather than envy those who have found it, why not take the route to joy that begins right in our own hands, knees, arms, and lungs? Dancing uses the master keys of grace, making, and fun. The adventure of moving into life's deeper waters is made confident and possible by entering through the door of joyfulness.

※ ❖ ※

CHAPTER FOUR

DANCING INTO WHOLENESS

"When the going gets tough, the tough go dancing."
—Eugene Robinson

My mom has Alzheimer's disease. Usually on my visits we sit on the couch and watch TV or go on excursions. Her language skills are a challenge. On a recent trip, sitting next to her, I played the soundtrack from a popular movie, and the contagious beat got me bouncing. Mom jumped right in. On the couch, grooving to the beat, her rhythm was impeccable. The dance was in her. Our hands joined, flirted, and played off each other. We giggled. I pulled her up off the couch. Five knee surgeries couldn't keep her down. She improvised turns and steps. I followed her lead. She matched me. I matched her. We laughed. If not for getting winded, she would have kept going. Dance changed both our worlds, for those few precious moments.

The power of dance is one of the hardest things to describe in words, which is probably why it's so poorly recorded in written history. Yet dance can sweep us into the complex interplay called wholeness, that mysterious, wild place that cannot be broken down. Movement can be a wonderful way to create course corrections for our lives, to shift from conflict to reconciliation, to retrieve lost aspects of ourselves, to claim what our body knows, and to develop inner strength. I've seen dance evoke great flow, joy, synchronicity, even ecstasy ... as long as perfectionism, complicated instructions, difficult steps, and bossy leaders didn't interfere. Dance is capable of restoring meaning when we feel lost and life seems meaninglessness, as a woman named Tziporah exclaimed: "I am lost ... so for now I will dance where I am, and love, and be." She realized that as long as she could sing and dance and live in her "wilderness," she was home.

Dancing quenches the restless heart. It's a way of acknowledging, integrating, even celebrating that we live in a world in constant motion. It's a way of unblocking self-expression. It's a way of breaking down barriers.

A dancer I know spoke in her church about relationships and the barriers we put up in order to feel safe and comfortable. She pointed out that people "tend to choose comfortable and known places to be, whether picking a familiar aisle and seat at the movie theater or 'our pew' at church." She then invited everyone to get up and move to a different place, to sit in a different pew. Even she was surprised when one of her sons came from the very back pew to sit in a pew right in front of her. "That service was one of the best ones we've had together," she said, "because we passed through some barriers that keep us apart."

Dancing is also a path that can lead us toward new ways of experiencing God. When Mary Louise McCullough led a movement experience at a retreat for clergywomen, she realized that "many of these women had never imagined moving and praying at the same time." After a simple danced meditation, many participants were in tears. Mary Louise knew that a change had occurred. She said, "I think this may have been an opening to the possibility of a nurturing, soft, creative God who arrives in our arms, legs, and bodyspirits when we move contemplatively."

The physical discoveries of dance often precede intellectual discoveries. When we are willing, our bodyspirits lead us to the Sacred in uncommon ways. I think of Victor Floyd, a man who usually sat behind a piano or sang opera. When he took a course on dance and prayer, he admitted, "I thought I did not dance. I sang and I organized music, happy and creative enough. Then a woman told me, 'You can dance.' Who *me*? I can do *what*? Dance? Let go? Be freer? Then, I just did it. [Now, I am] like a child with love handles, a child who doesn't mind being interesting, or strange, or plain, or bizarre, or wrong, or brilliant, or able to handle love." I got to see Victor dance. His effervescence spilled over into the space. It was a treat to encounter him in such fully embodied joy.

If you are used to sitting, conversing, and thinking things over, dance may challenge you in good ways. A manageable risk can refresh weary souls. I learned how true this is when a dear friend came to my graduate school class on dance and spirituality. She watched me cater to the fatigue of my students. Flopping down on the floor, weary and drained from their studies, these adults literally whined when I asked them to move. "Challenge them," my friend advised. So I did, and their energy surged.

Sometimes, listening to the exhaustion of our bodies and dropping to the floor is warranted. But other times, we need to move past what's holding us back and start from a new vantage point. Our dancing bodies can give us a foundation for a more energizing wholeness. Instead of trying so hard to balance our activities with rest, what if we let our body wisdom guide us through every part of our day? It turns out that it is much easier to find integration by starting with our body and including our mind than it is to start with our mind and attempt to include our body.

Dancing can also expand our sense of wholeness. When we narrow ourselves to the security we feel in areas where we are gifted or comfortable, our wholeness is diminished. If we don't develop a full palette of mental, emotional, and spiritual health, sometimes entire areas of development get left off our menu. I think of Socrates, who learned to dance when he was seventy because he felt that an essential part of him had been neglected. In a similar way, I often joke that the right, creative side of my brain got so big that I had to carry it around in a sling. What about my verbal, analytical side? I need my whole brain, fully engaged, to really do the dance of life.

I like to think of dance as an open, spacious boat that can carry all parts of us as we move over the oceans and rivers of life. Our bodyspirit wants to feel buoyed, and dance is a boat that can do that. Dancing transports our diverse forms of intelligence and helps us to be fully human, fully alive, and good at changing and growing.

In the 1980s, psychologist Dr. Howard Gardner developed the theory that, instead of only one kind of intelligence, we actually have multiple intelligences and, therefore, multiple ways of learning. His theory has affected educators everywhere, helping people identify and honor their individual strengths. In the United Kingdom, the Birmingham Grid for Learning adapted Gardner's intelligence categories for a standardized test to help people discover which forms of intelligence are their strongest. It is very interesting to note that body wisdom—"kinesthetic intelligence"—is at the top of the list.

> Kinesthetic: Body Smart
> Linguistic: Word Smart
> Logical: Number Smart
> Interpersonal: People Smart
> Intrapersonal: Myself Smart
> Musical: Music Smart
> Visual/Spatial: Picture Smart
> Naturalistic: Nature Smart

When I read the online results of nearly half a million people who took the test in the UK, I saw that Body Smarts and People

Smarts ranked highest. Considering the insignificant role that the body generally plays in traditional educational and religious practices in England and throughout the Western world, I have to wonder why so many people's needs and strengths are being passed over. With the kinesthetic, bodily intelligence of countless people so impoverished, we would surely derive great benefit from reintegrating our body wisdom back into life. I believe that many people, especially the young, already do this, as seen in the ever increasing popularity of Eastern spiritual practices like chi gong, yoga, and t'ai chi.

"Wholeness" is a much-sought-after quality these days, whether we're talking about whole foods, health, or quality of life. People are searching for a sense of peace, for balance, for an awakening, for new possibilities. The "Body Smarts" found in dancing have the potential to carry us from anxious to peaceful, from ordinary to extraordinary, from out of balance to balanced, from held back to liberated—changes that a lot of us feel are long overdue.

Anxious to Peaceful

Ambitious peaceseekers go to great lengths to find inner peace, sitting in multiday meditations, taking long retreats, and spending precious income on spa treatments and home entertainment. What if peace were closer and easier than we imagined? Denise Dunbar-Winton attended a retreat in Yamba, Australia, where a hand dance was all it took to help her find peace and connect to Spirit. She describes her response in a poem called "Spirited Hand Dance":

Music entered me

Through every pore
In a pulsing sweet osmosis.
Slowly I opened my palm

And held it, as it held me.
Note by note, I lifted it,
Observed, and caressed it,
Moved around and through it
And its rhythm became my own.

I played with it, and it with me
As we swelled and subsided,
Rose and fell,
We danced an embrace
Then glided apart,
We paused in midair
Then tumbled and rolled like a laugh.

As we rested, suspended and weightless,
I became the harmony,
Its beat became my heart.
I breathed in my hand dance in Spirit
And wanted nothing more, and nothing less.
I'd been inspired
And was fulfilled.

A hand dance for greater peace is as easy as eating ripe fruit off a tree. Try it and see.

Dancing Two Minutes of Heaven, Therapy, or Just Vacation

~ Put on some peaceful music and lie down in a comfortable position.

~ Move your arm through the air like seaweed suspended in water being sloshed back and forth by gentle waves.

~ Move one of your arms fast, then slow, then jerky, then smooth.

~ Let your arm hang above you like the limb of a tree.

~ Let your arm relax and make contact with your body or the ground.

~ Include your other arm as you let both arms dance.

~ When the music ends, as you lie quietly, reflect on the peace that surrounds you.

~ Embrace and savor the gift of the present moment.

❖ ❖ ❖

When I lead this exercise with a roomful of people, I see the way that movement like this "disarms" us. No one seems to notice anyone else. Each individual seems completely absorbed in the activity. A few lie motionless. Occasionally, people fall asleep—something they probably need more than enlightenment. Most are still moving when the music ends, their bodies having dropped the whirl of duty and social pretense. With the tensions melted, participants sometimes tap into a secret source of restoration. Even children enjoy this kind of meditation.

Another way to move from a state of anxiety to a state of peace is as simple as shaking. I use a playful shaking sequence to help groups let go of tension. Most of the time, people already know they are "full of it" (tension) and are more than happy to let it go. Just ten seconds of shaking helps.

Shake It Out

~ Shake out one hand.

~ Shake out the other hand.

~ Shake a leg.

~ Shake out the other leg.

~ Shake out your middle.

~ Shake out your bottom, and whatever you're "metaphorically" sitting on.

~ Shake out your voice.

~ Take a deep breath and let it out with a sigh … *ahhhh.*

❖ ❖ ❖

Dr. James Gordon, a leader in the field of integrative medicine, believes that pairing shaking and dancing "can energize your depressed body, relieve your preoccupied mind, and dissolve your tension. It can also, as you do it regularly, help you feel more at home in your body, and bring you into the moment-to-moment flow of your life." Shaking is not meant to please the eye. (Although, if you watch African dancers, rock-concert attendees, or kids on the street doing hip-hop, there is great delight to be had in rattling our bodies.) Shaking is all about releasing and rebalancing biological systems.

Psychotherapist and ethnographer Bradford Keeney promotes shaking, too. He studies what he calls "shaking medicine" among Minnesota Ojibwa Indians, Japanese practitioners of Seiku Jutsu, and the Kalahari bushmen, who all shake for healing, refreshment, and ecstatic communion. In his book *Shaking Medicine*, Keeney observes that when people "fall into the shake," they find themselves, "maybe for the first time, in the kindergarten of ecstatic experience." He writes, "Heightened arousal—whether through free movement, spontaneous jumping, or body shaking—is as valuable a transformative experience as sitting quietly in a lotus position."

Rather than trying to "control" your anxiety, the next time you find yourself feeling anxious, or fretting about something over which you have no control, or simply feeling "wound up," let your body help you release the tension. When you come home from a particularly difficult day, shaking can help you release the day's stresses and make room for "the peace that passes understanding" (Philippians 4:7) to fill body and mind.

Spirit Shaker

1. Put one hand in the other. Bend your elbows and bring your hands close to your chest, as if you were holding dice. Vigorously shake your hands.

2. Say *ahhhh* as you shake and let the vibrations move from the inside out.

3. Unclasp your hands and continue shaking each of them, along with your limbs, letting breath and vocalization join in.

4. Move into pulsing, bobbing, clapping, and stomping at your current energy level.

5. Add rhythmic music if you like, and let yourself dance freely.

6. As you "let go and let God," surrender anything you want to your Higher Power. If this becomes ecstatic, welcome the joy it offers you.

7. As you cool down, let your breathing grow quiet again, entering the calm after a storm.

8. When you finish, notice how your body is feeling. Has your energy shifted? Have your thoughts gone in a new direction from when you started? If you are keeping a dance journal, take a few minutes to record your experience.

❖ ❖ ❖

ORDINARY TO EXTRAORDINARY

Dancing can dramatically shift our experiences of time and space. Choreographer Agnes de Mille once said, "To dance is to be out of yourself, larger, more beautiful, more powerful." People who dance lose track of time. They dance through the night as their brains release the "no time like the present" chemicals that give them a "high."

Time and *space* are ways to name certain kinds of awareness. While we may loosely describe ourselves as feeling "down, spacey, open, or not-all-here," some cultures have more sophisticated means to differentiate among such states. The Greeks identify time that is ruled by calendars and clocks as *chronos* time, and expansive "fullness of time," where we have "all the time in the world," as *kairos* time. Ruth St. Denis found her *kairos* when she was moving. She said, "In those moments when I am dancing, I am beyond time and space."

When I am dancing inside the walls of my studio, I can hear sirens, traffic, and pedestrians pass by. I'm less than fifteen feet from the street, yet I'm in a world of music, beauty, and movement. Sometimes I ask myself, "Which space is the real one?"

Many humans crave "expansive states." We seek spiritual teachers who will encourage us to pray, open ourselves to the Divine, and bring back the gifts of expansiveness to our everyday living. Popular spiritual sayings, like "The kingdom of heaven is within you" or "Enlightenment is here and now," convey the malleability of time and space. If you visit "trance dance" sites on the Internet, you'll find thousands of people practicing transpersonal technologies to help them enter mind-altering states.

While we may long for moments of transcendence, we are limited by our all-too human hesitation to engage them. I remember how thrilled my daughter was to attend her first middle-school dance.

"How was the dance?" I asked her afterwards.

"Boring," she replied with disappointment.

The problem? Few of the students were dancing. With typical adolescent confusion about peer acceptance and sexuality, they spent more time clinging to the walls than following their instincts for fun and community. They wanted to "play" but were trapped by their own social constraints.

Maybe you've heard the story of Jill Bolte Taylor, a brain researcher who had a stroke that opened her to the larger dance of life. When she told her story—which originally appeared in *O, The Oprah Magazine*—to hundreds of technology, entertainment, and design experts, they gave her a standing ovation. Listen to how she described her world after having her stroke:

The absence of experience is bliss. It was peaceful and beautiful there. I was with God … I could see that my spirit was huge. I didn't see how I would be able to squeeze myself back into this tiny little body. All details of my life and language were gone. Language is a kind of code, and things were no longer reduced to coding. I was looking at the big picture and could see how everything is related. Everything is in motion, connected in a dance of grace. The brain is what imposes boundaries, and boundaries convey a perception of separation, but that's a delusion. Everything is one.

When I read her story, I broke into tears. My brother had had two strokes when we were growing up. I was barely a teenager when he and my family felt the profound effect of the tiny rupture of one of his blood vessels. His loss of movement and his brush with death were horrifying. Yet here was Jill throwing divine light on my terror as one who had journeyed through her stroke, survived, and received the greatest blessing—intimacy with God. She blew me away. As soon as I finished reading her article, I wrote to thank her. She responded and confirmed that her experience felt closer to singing and dancing than anything else. In fact, her website refers to her as a "singing scientist."

This gives a little glimpse of what it is like when we get beyond the limits of what we are told is the "proper" way to dance, or the "right" way to move, and become fully engaged in the experience of dancing. As Jill realized, "Everything is in motion, connected in a dance of grace." Movement can shift us beyond enculturation so we can get in touch with the "big picture." Hopefully, we don't have to have a stroke to discover this. Dance can lead us to this space of *kairos* time and God.

Another wise teacher, Richard Strozzi-Heckler, a somatic leadership coach, describes a similar paradox where "the deeper we descend into the body, the less we are attached to it. We find we are many bodies. We realize we are no body." He believes that it is through developing this kind of awareness that "we become more effective in how we care for others and the planet."

Detachment can be a spacious experience. It is a state of being neither super body-conscious nor body-denying. Teachers like Strozzi-Heckler are needed to remind us about this generous reality, since we forget it as we focus on the business that's right in our face. Clocking in and out of work, picking up kids when they get out of school, showing up for that interview, paying attention to deadlines and due dates—all these define our days. Even theater tickets and worship services go by the clock. None of this is bad. Being "on time" is respectful to others. But, left to our own devices, parts of us beg to go "off the clock." Dancing is one of the quickest, most efficient ways to shift to the mini-Sabbath of *kairos* time.

When dancing creates detachment, it can awaken a spacious, loving, compassionate connection to the world and God. Transcending ego, moving beyond the more mundane limits of our physical bodies, we meet creation. We sense a call to something bigger.

Off-the-Clock Dance

~ Do you know what time it is? Notice the clock.

~ Walk in any direction, moving in serpentine fashion. As you count to sixty, move to a steady beat for about a minute.

~ Keep moving in cadence if being in this kind of *chronos* time feels like dancing.

~ Now put on some music. When you are ready, switch to some "fake t'ai chi" moves (slow, smooth movements).

~ Glide through space. Open, extend, and stretch your limbs as you play with the space. Imagine dancing with the stars or a loved one in a far-off place.

~ Let this meditation stretch out for as long as you like.

~ When you come to an end, take a deep breath and let it out with a sigh.

~ Squirm around to come back to the present moment.

~ Notice the clock again.

~ How does playing with time and space expand, limit, or connect you to a bigger reality?

❖ ❖ ❖

OUT OF BALANCE TO BALANCED

There was a time when I took a break from performing. I'd lost my taste for it. When I rejoined my performing group, I was struck by a new agility, ease, and balance in my body. Standing on one leg, I could swing the other without any wobbles. Moving felt like singing a beloved old tune. I ran around the room, spun, and caught myself suspended on one leg. None of it was planned. I was dancing for joy.

Balance is easier when you don't care, worry, or try to over-control yourself. Why? Because physical balance is happening all the time, and we're good at it. Our muscles play imperceptible games of tug-of-war between one side and the other. Weight constantly shifts when we stand, walk, and move. If we try to control our balance, pulling ourselves onto the head of an imaginary pin, balance gets harder. It only improves as we relax, expand, and settle into the earth.

Similarly, dance as a spiritual practice can help us move from being tightly wound to more easygoing. How? Because the physical lesson of balance is also spiritual: Staying balanced isn't a matter of staying rigidly in one spot. Dancing requires quick changes in positioning, especially in our feet, ankles, knees, and hips. We find balance by continually making subtle adjustments.

One teacher keeps reminding me to wear my spiritual practice like a loose-fitting garment. As one who takes God very seriously, I tend to overcontrol things. If I move and breathe around my beliefs and disciplines, as I must when I am dancing, they actually work better for me. Clinging to them is stunting. In this regard, dancing serves as one of my spiritual directors, informing me of my current tightness or ease, my capacity to surrender or to insist on control.

One secret of balancing is to increase our range of motion. While that might seem counterintuitive (we might be more inclined to decrease our moves to try to stay balanced), widening our base of operating can be an enormous help. Think of how you stand. Put your feet ankle to ankle, and you'll feel wobbly, but increase the space between your feet and you will feel comfortable and strong. Alternatively, if we increase our range of movement *too* much, we also lose balance. Each of us needs to find the right range of motion for ourselves.

Movement educators like Gabrielle Roth show us the way out of narrow control ruts and back to full balance. She developed her 5Rhythms™ method based on what she describes as the five sacred rhythms that are the essence of the body: flowing, staccato, chaos, lyrical, and stillness. Another system, Laban Movement Analysis, teaches the use of effort through eight combinations descriptively named float, punch (thrust), glide, slash, dab, wring, flick, and press. A ninth quality, flow, refers to the "ongoing-ness" of our motions.

Kinesiologists Judith Rathbone and Valerie Hunt scientifically uncovered four kinesthetic "home bases" that came to be called swing, thrust, shape, and hang. Observing and testing dancers and athletes, these two women realized that each individual works from a unique combination of kinesthetic patterning. They recognized that individual diversity is, indeed, more than skin deep. It begins at birth in the ways the neurons in our muscles fire. Each dancer's strong and weak patterning makes her the kind of mover and person and spirit she is, that unique energetic essence that others see in our bodies.

Those who have investigated the four patterns have found that when we celebrate and build on our "home base," it generates energy and inspiration, or what I call grace. You might find it very interesting to know that when dance educator Betsy Wetzig explored these four patterns and observed, with Ginny Whitelaw, how these patterns influence the way people lead, they found that drivers "thrust," visionaries "hang," collaborators "swing," and organizers "shape."

If energy has anything to do with spirit, which I believe it does, then repressing our "home style" (or the style of other people) negatively affects our overall health and our ability to foster grace. If we're uncomfortable with our style (or unaware of it), we will have trouble embracing it, let alone balancing it.

To my chagrin, I found that I'm a thruster. When I realized this, it was as if every light in my inner house flipped on. I'd been taught to be friendly, cooperative, nice, and to give way to others—especially men. Even as I attempted to shape my behaviors along these lines, I developed strange jabbing compulsions and frustrating habits of risk taking and overwork. Without intending to, I became increasingly passive-aggressive. I was out of balance. I didn't know how to claim "thrusting," in my spirituality, much less in my role as a mother, wife, and teacher. It never occurred to me that the very movement pattern I was fighting was my home base. I had no models of healthy thrusting.

When I began to work with thrusting movements, what surprised me most was learning that thrusting produces immediate relaxation in the muscles of a thruster and, at the same time, energizes. Pushing, pulling, and focused muscularity usher in the thruster's joy and peace. If you hold a thruster down, he becomes drained. "Sit still" is an invitation to tense up. As I experimented, I immediately found this to be true. This revelation changed my life. Learning that thrusting was my God-given kinesthetic path, I began to see my energy as that of an athlete. Instead of repressing myself, I wondered how thrusting could figure in and illuminate my spiritual path as well.

I met a man who was the last in a line of Tibetan oracle dancers. He was lovely, kind, and had a radiant smile … until he took on his oracle role. That is when he functioned in another spirit altogether. To loud clangs of gong and percussion, he chased away evil spirits by thrusting, jumping, and sticking out his tongue.

In Sierra Leone, West Africa, I'd seen similar energy in the Bundu spirit dancer. The raffia-covered, masked dancer entered the circle of community and began to poke the air with joy during a sacred dance ceremony in honor of the initiation of several young women. It was a dance of protection, power, and blessing.

I needed a female model, a Greek goddess, an Athena or a Diana; or Hawaii's goddess of fire, Pele; or the Hindu goddess Kali, who stands with one foot on Shiva's chest, her enormous tongue sticking out, a sword in one hand, the head of a demon in another, and her two other hands blessing her worshippers, saying, "Fear not!" To restore my wholeness, I began to revise my idea of a feminine spirituality, which allowed me to celebrate thrust in my movement practices.

Instead of holding myself in, I began to open up my body and let vigor dance. This increased my joy. I felt giddy and powerful all at once as long as I followed one cardinal rule: Never thrust in anger at another person. It took time and commitment to master this nonviolent practice, but today my values and physicality feel blessedly integrated. I have both my spiritual and physical power and my relationship to the Holy. At the same time, it has become easier for me to incorporate into my dancing the other kinesthetic movements of swing, hang, and shape.

Finding your own "home base" is an important part of finding your balance. The exercises below will take you through the four styles of movement: swing, thrust, shape, and hang. Give each a try and then take time to journal about your response to the different movements.

Moving to "Home Base"

Before each movement pattern, take a deep breath, sigh, and shake yourself out.

SWING

1. Start by rocking or swaying.
2. Swing your hips.
3. Swing your arms. Front to back. Side to side. Swing high, low, fast, slow. Let the momentum of the movement carry you.
4. Swinging is like sweeping. As you "sweep," imagine clearing away thoughts, projects, or concerns that you don't need to entertain right now.
5. If you are with another person, swing her around.
6. Twirl, spin, bounce, or jump.
7. At rest, notice your energy.

Take a deep breath, sigh, and shake yourself out.

THRUST

1. Ground yourself in the earth and gather your energy to your center.
2. Imagine that you are a Sumo wrestler. Engage your arm muscles as if you were pushing and pulling against an outside force. Notice your energy.
3. Next, imagine throwing paint on the wall, flinging out the accumulation of the day, the joy and the frustration. Make sounds that match your movement. It won't feel half as good if you try to hold your breath. Including breath and voice improves this movement exponentially.

4. Try thirty seconds of "fake tap dancing." Let your feet and arms make percussive strikes and swishes on the floor as you pretend to be Fred Astaire or Ginger Rogers, summoning the spirituality of delight.
5. Do thirty seconds of "fake flamenco," a vertical, stomping, and poised dance to activate your grounded spiritual passion.
6. Do ten seconds of "fake karate" with quick, focused martial-art moves to release your energy and call up your power, courage, and action.

Take a deep breath, sigh, and shake yourself out.

SHAPE

1. Place yourself in a shape. Rest in the contained stillness.
2. Create a series of different shapes, welcoming stillness as you sense the line and dimension of your body.
3. Shift from shape to shape with crisp energy, increasing or decreasing the lengths of stillness.
4. Stretching, engage your muscles as you move through posture-like shapes. Notice the qualities of yoga, ballet, and hand mudras in the shapes you visit.
5. Relax your attention on the shapes you make, and begin to let your shapes carry you, like frames in a movie.

Take a deep breath, sigh, and shake yourself out.

HANG

1. While standing, let your weight drop into the ground. Stand easy on your feet. Imagine being a little drunk. Fall a little in any direction, letting momentum carry you for a few a steps.
2. Float with your arms as if you were snorkeling, hanging in a pool of water like a fish, or suspended on an air current like a bird.

3. Using slow, smooth "fake t'ai chi" moves, soothe your energies and gather them back to the vicinity of your body. Let your attention and awareness follow the feelings of weight and energy. Go with the flow.

Take a deep breath, sigh, and shake yourself out.

INTEGRATE

~ To end, move any way you want, drawing on any of these movement patterns, or forget them altogether and move as you wish.

~ Now take a few minutes to journal about what you noticed for each of the four movements.

~ Where did you feel the most ease?

~ Which movement gave you energy?

~ Which movement felt demanding?

~ Where did you feel resistant?

~ How do you think these movements relate to what you want more or less of in life?

~ What movement most nourishes your physicality of grace today?

Come back, practice, and play with these movements again in the future. Here are some additional questions to ponder as you continue your practice:

~ Can you embrace the "spirit" of each way of moving as sacred? Each pattern has sacred expressions. For instance, swinging is inherent in sacred hula, circle dances, and dervish dancing. Shaping is at the heart of ballet, sitting meditation, yoga, and the Indian classical dance Bharathanatyam. African dance and New Zealander Maori dancing incorporate thrusting in their sacred practices. Hanging appears in the earthed, repetitive, communal steps of North American Indian tribal dances and ecstatic dances.

~ What areas of sacred movement might you be ready to explore?

~ Could you bring more balance to body and soul through these patterns?

When you swing:

~ Where is your center? Do you sense strength and grounding there?

~ How does swinging back and forth deepen reciprocity and your sense of give-and-take?

~ What is it like to play with different sides of you? With more than one direction to go? How does your comfort or discomfort with this relate to your life with others and with the Divine?

When you thrust:

~ Can you focus your energy and power? Can you send it out?

~ Can you differentiate between violent and powerful?

~ How much or how little do you want to do this?

~ Do you like to push and pull?

~ Is it fun to let go in big, active movements?

When you shape:

~ How easy or difficult is it to hold a shape for a while? Do you like the stillness?

~ Do you enjoy being in a place with nothing else to do or be?

~ Do you enjoy creating and placing your shapes?

~ How easy or difficult is it for you let go of shapes and just flow?

~ As you move from position to position, is it easy to be definite and clear, or do you tend to blur and merge the movements?

When you hang:

~ How easy or difficult is it for you to flop, flail, or drop your weight as though it didn't matter?

~ How do you think your ease or difficulty with this movement relates to your ability to do nothing, hang out, and enjoy?

Combining movements:

~ Try moving back and forth between directing energy (thrusting) and going with the flow (hanging).

~ Try swinging and then shaping your movement.

~ As you find ease in combining the different movement types, make note of any shifts in your physical and spiritual balance.

❖ ❖ ❖

HELD BACK TO LIBERATED

The opposite of being in balance is falling. Would you believe that learning to fall is liberating? Fall down. Go boom. Get up. Go on.

When was the last time you fell? What were you thinking or feeling? One winter while teaching at Whitworth University in Spokane, Washington, as I carefully stepped through the snow, I lost my footing. I wasn't used to ice and snow, and in spite of feeling protective of a painful cyst in my wrist, as the icy ground rose up to meet me, my hands flew out. I landed square, both wrists fully flexed. What a shock when the impact busted open the nodule in my wrist. When I stood back up, I exclaimed, "The pain! It's gone!" The restrictive pain in my wrist had completely vanished. Falling was my healer! As a dancer, I had obviously fallen down many times. I'd even broken a metatarsal in my foot in one dance. But this was the first time that falling had broken open something more than pride. Intuition told me that this could be true in other ways. I began to think differently about falling.

I sometimes watch *America's Funniest Home Videos* on television. The most thrilling, devastating, amazing sequences are those of people flying through the air on skateboards, bicycles, skis, and skates to ballet music. Their abandon is exhilarating. Their devastating disasters make me gasp or groan. This is *not* the kind of fall I am talking about.

There are over fifty definitions of *fall* in the dictionary, including "descend," "drop," "land forcibly," "be wounded or killed in battle," "come down in ruins," "lose power, lose status, fall afoul, fall among, fall away, fall flat, fall from grace." These feature "going down" in big ways. Falling hurts! We spend the first years of life confirming this fact: skinned knees, scraped elbows, red faces. As we age, our fear of falling begins to overtake our daring, and we learn to hold back instead of fully flinging ourselves into life. Then one day, it's clear. Avoid falling! Down with pain! Up with balance! At all costs! Balance the books, balance relationships, balance your diet, schedule, family, and career.

Strangely, the universe keeps insisting that we fall and get up. It presents us with its unavoidable gravitas. When we get out of bed in the morning, instead of ascending into the heavens, our feet hit the floor, and we begin our daily dance of getting up and getting let down. We think that we are going to sit in a chair, but in order to put our rear ends on the cushion, we have to agree to fall. This is even more obvious when we contrast our adult view with that of kids, who don't care about throwing themselves onto couches or floors. In aging, as our belly strength weakens, we begin to aim ourselves in the right direction, groan, and let gravity do the rest of the work. In time, many elders learn to respect the inevitable conclusion of our dance on earth. This body is going down.

WILL WE BEFRIEND OUR "FALL" OR DESPISE IT?

Twentieth-century hymn writer Brian Wren, who studied with a dancer, was moved by the fact that "after demonstrating a falling movement, she [the teacher] said that while some artists have things to hide behind [the preacher behind the pulpit, the cellist behind the cello, the actor behind the role], a dancer has no hiding place; what you see is what you get." He published a hymn to honor the poignancy of our human condition and the quality of our rising up, the little resurrections demonstrated by those who move with grace.

If we want to fly, to know liberation of body and soul, we must embrace the earth—or at least relax our fears of fall and failure. In my twenties I choreographed a dance I called "Falling" to the chant of the twelfth-century abbess Hildegard of Bingen. I had begun recognizing my desire to look morally good at all costs. I created "Falling" as a spiritual inquiry into my inherited and personal dynamics. Something in my body seemed to forever insist on "rising above" my own humanity and that of other people. I sensed that this prideful, nose in the air, chin up, everything up, up, up was quickly becoming a spiritual roadblock.

In a studio, as I moved to Hildegard's glorious spiritual music, I learned that literally reaching toward heaven made my falls to earth more dramatic and intense. I would reach all the way up onto the balls of my feet, my arms extended, my chest hanging onto the sky, proud of feeling so secure on one leg, and then plunge to the floor. When my colleague Phil watched me practice, he said I still looked too controlled, too careful, not real enough. Furiously, I threw myself to the floor again and again, intent on making my falls look real. This dance became a rite of initiation that helped me integrate gravity and falling into life. As a people-pleasing, up-and-at-'em person, I knew that finding my balance required finding the ground of my being.

One day a Jesuit priest saw me do this falling dance and shared his reflections in a letter to me: "Tears welled up and I could not speak about it afterwards. You must really know intimately the movements of prayer and longing for God, and the struggle for oneness with God, and the depths of sorrow and pain and loss in falling, in day-to-day falling or otherwise, of the grace that can be brought to falling once you learn to embrace it."

Our need for balance is only part of a much greater struggle in spiritual life. We also need to learn that, when we fall, we can get up again. Listen for a moment to this early Christian story taken from the Desert Fathers:

> A monk traveled a long way to seek advice from a Desert Father. He traveled for days and days and finally came to the hut of Abba Sisoes.
>
> "Father, Father!" exclaimed the monk, "I found you! I need your help, for I have fallen!"
>
> Abba Sisoes studied the young monk and said, "Get up!"
>
> Taken aback, expecting better advice than this, the young monk said, "You don't understand, Abba, I sinned. I have fallen!"
>
> The Desert Father said again, "Get up!"
>
> Frustrated and sad about his failure to live a truly holy life, the young man demanded, "Father, please! You must tell me what to do!'
>
> The Desert Father said, "There is nothing to do except to get up, get up, and get up until you are taken up either in sin or in virtue."

There's an ironic thing about falling: If we practice falling, learning to give in to it, we are rewarded with moments of liberation. Jeanette Stokes, a leader in women's spirituality, was in her forties when she joined an improvisational dance troupe. Once, she lined up three guys, ran toward them, and flung herself into their arms. She did it three times. The last time, a man swung her around. It was a moment of sheer liberation. Fear of falling gave birth to a dance of flight. Dancing gradually taught her to trust her body and her ability to recover from all manner of clumsiness. She said, "I don't like falling, in dancing or in life. It scares me. I seem to have done a lot of it in recent years. Falling out of a marriage, falling out of relationships, falling down on the job. I still don't like it, but now I do it without getting as banged up as I used to." I might add, she is having more fun, too.

Falling requires trust, and trust comes step-by-step as we learn the ways of our own body and soul. Knowing what we can do in any given moment, and working well with whatever limits and possibilities there are, we restore grace, freedom, and balance to the dance of life.

In his classic *All I Really Need to Know I Learned in Kindergarten*, Robert Fulghum wrote that kindergarten wisdom invites us to "live a balanced life—learn some and think some and draw and paint and sing and dance and play and work every day some." I'm glad he included dance! Dance is a way of coming to life, of learning to enjoy the unabashed fullness of our spiritual life.

If you are feeling bound by "shoulds," fearful of making a mistake, tired of hanging onto something (or someone) too tightly, maybe it's time to play with a little falling. Maybe it's time to let yourself feel the liberation of letting go of upright rigidity and allow gravity to bring you home. Perhaps it's time to stop trying so hard to be "graceful" and let yourself just be yourself. I offer this practice of "Falling for Liberation" as a bodily experience of the spiritual lessons of falling, of both the freedom to let go and the resilience to get up again, and again.

Falling for Liberation

1. Find a "friendly" floor, soft couch, or bed. Seated, gently fall in different ways, slowly, to the side, to the back, using your arms in different ways. (Do this exercise where you will be safe. You don't want to add to your fear of falling!)

2. Having fallen, lie on the floor, couch, or bed for a minute, noticing how it holds you. Notice what it's like to get up, to rise again.

3. You may want to try falling from higher up. Go to your knees. Fall, and get up.

4. Now put on music and practice falling, resting, rising to honor—instead of trying to resist—gravity.

5. Perhaps you want to stay close to the floor rather than falling again and again from a higher position. If this is the case, use the floor as your base. As you lie down, push yourself up, spin, suspend, and relax again. Using the support of the floor, pretend to fly. This can be one of the best workouts of your day, but it can also be a spiritual exercise.

6. Reflect for a few minutes, or write in your journal about sensations while falling and rising. How do these small "recoveries" compare to getting over other difficulties? If you can get up in your body, perhaps you can get up from your hardships, too. Can you imagine God supporting you at each part of your rising and falling?

❖ ❖ ❖

It is liberating to breathe, shake, move, balance, fall off balance, tense and release, liberate our wholeness. We don't have to hide the truth. We can dance it! To quote Iraneaus, "The glory of God is a human being fully alive." Thank heaven, he didn't say "perfect"!

CHAPTER FIVE

DANCING FOR HEALING

"Things are losing their hardness.
Now even my body lets the light through."
—Virginia Woolf

I've had a lot of healing to do. It's not so much that I *had* to do it; it's that I wanted happiness; I wanted to feel free, to love God, to dance, and to offer my best to others. Ancestral anxieties, personal wounds, absences of entire areas of expression haunted me. For instance, I couldn't talk with ease. Whenever I talked, it was as if someone were beaming an interrogation light on me. My thoughts got thick and my speech was stilted.

There were other challenges. I had no sense of rhythm, which is odd and disconcerting for a dancer. I also excelled at repressing anxiety and shame. Some might consider this fortunate, but what it meant was that I had to be either a really "good girl" or insanely defensive. To avoid anxiety, I had to run around and do a lot of things for people.

I once wrote a poem to take account of some of the other things I thought I would never do, things that with healing became possible.

> I hated to cook.
> But now I'm in the kitchen
> flippin' burgers.

I was afraid to speak.
But now I preach without warning.

I couldn't sit still.
But now I might befriend
the Dalai Lama.

I couldn't keep from asking
How are you?
Now I just say Good Day.

I spent money I didn't have.
Now I balance my checkbook.

Once I always had to go.
But now I am home
and happy.

In all ways, dancing supported my healing again and again. It gave me a way to befriend the unbefriendable, to coax hidden parts of body and soul from the shadows, to choose experiences from the menu of life that I had no exposure to, and to retrieve parts of myself that got frightened off. Dancing is a beautiful way to heal. By choosing to dance as a sacred art, it is likely that, as we encounter difficulty in life, dancing will do its job like a multivitamin, bolstering our spiritual immune system and renewing gladness for being the body we are.

I know that when I am grieved and in turmoil, if I remember to dance, to unleash my creative energy, though the results may not be beautiful or worth showing, the work of my soul will restore me to wholeness.

Everyone needs healing. But what is the healing we need? As one poet wondered, "Who knows what ritual will bring relief?" Different kinds of wounding require different bodyspirit strategies.

If you feel scattered, overwhelmed, and tired, it's time for a dance of restoration.

If you feel as if you've forgotten how to jump-start joy and love or you've lost your sense of humor and playfulness, you might benefit from a "shadow" dance, engaging parts of life stuck in the shadows.

If you're feeling stressed to the point of shutting down because of the insanity of life, this requires a dance of "exformation," letting go of energies and ideas that have you physically bound up.

If you've experienced a sudden shock, change, or trauma, accompanied by lethargy or lack of desire to move, sing, talk, or connect, this form of soul loss calls for a dance of soul retrieval.

SELF-CARE: DANCING FOR RESTORATION

To dance quickens serenity and stillness.

To dance to your own muse increases energy.

To dance is to breathe with your soul.

Sandra Ingerman, author of *Soul Retrieval: Mending the Fragmented Self*, defines *soul* as "our essence, life force, the part of our vitality that keeps us alive and thriving." Most religions view soul as the unified, perceivable, intangible, yet vulnerable spirit or psyche. In Hebrew the soul is *nefesh*, that which breathes. Jewish mystics believe soul encompasses *ruach*, "moral virtues and the ability to distinguish between good and evil," and *neshamah*, the higher self, related to the intellect, which in death returns to the Source, where it enjoys "the kiss of the beloved."

To lose soul is dire. Yet healers know that this loss can happen even gradually, on an everyday level. When daily struggles get to us, our spiritual immune system easily weakens. We're scattered, at loose ends, empty. With too few opportunities to sing, dance, and tell our stories—activities that were once woven into the fabric of village life—the light of our soul force can dim.

Dorothy Morrison and Kristin Madden, authors of *Dancing the Goddess Incarnate: Living the Magic of Maiden, Mother and Crone*, describe the long-term impact of soul loss: "Our bodies stop moving as they once did and we pay the price for it as we age. This blocked self-expression results in energy blockages that continue to affect our actions and bodies forever—unless we regain the courage to dance."

The inevitability of a diminished soul is one reason that spiritual teachers direct us to the wisdom of children. Kids demonstrate soul force in full-bodied, free-spirited openness. Sacred teachers aren't suggesting that we become immature; rather, they are inviting us to stay open to life in its fullness. Some of us reconnect to our original innocence by playing with children or grandchildren. Kids can even get us to dance again.

Easygoing movement rituals can help us retrieve our fragmented energies from encounters in the harried, chaotic world. Daily, weekly, monthly practices can restore our loving, wise, spirited physicality. Early Church father St. Augustine honored dance as a way to restore health. He said, "I praise the dance, for it frees people from the heaviness of matter and binds the isolated to community.... Dance is a transformation of space, of time, of people, who are in constant danger of becoming all brain, will, or feeling."

Dancing reconnects many of us with our deepest selves, with our true feelings. Martha Graham, who choreographed the Greek Tragedies, believed that "movement never lies. It is a barometer telling the state of the soul's weather." I believe this is why some people cry when they start dancing again. A few realize that they never even danced as children. Beautiful experiences in movement awaited them all this time, and yet they avoided dance, treated it as strange, or were restricted from it. When they begin to move, they realize how much they have lost.

I also believe that some people would rather not get in touch with what is really going on, at their core, and for that very reason refuse to dance.

A beautiful woman, living at home in a restrictive religious family, discovered InterPlay. She had so much enthusiasm and energy for life, her face lit up the room. She could have been an actress or a spiritual leader, yet her community denigrated her playfulness and constantly reminded her to bow her head and work. Her family could not understand her irrepressible spirit. They blamed her for refusing to grow up. In the process she became ill. When she finally "escaped" to an InterPlay workshop and could dance and sing, she wept. She could hardly believe that her gifts were welcome. Returning home to her family, she began to find sneaky ways to let her spirit dance. At her computer, hiding her hands beneath her desk, she takes surreptitious hand dance breaks. The bathroom has become her sanctuary, her studio, the only safe place she has to sing, dance, and restore her soul.

For those who are kinesthetically sensitive, dancing may be especially crucial for self-care. I know. I pick up emotions so easily, I have to avoid scary movies. Other people's agendas swamp me. Things throw me out of balance (some would say, out of my body) on a daily basis. I've learned that to keep my verve, ardor, and health amid the daily bangs and bumps, recessions and inflations of life, I need to keep dancing. To do what is good for me, amid work, family needs, household tasks, and other commitments, I need to consciously, prayerfully dance at least once a week. Even in tough times, dancing grounds me, clears me, and keeps me connected to my body. Moving, vocalizing, telling my story, receiving contact, and just being with others—the five recommended daily requirements for healthy living—save me from depression, confusion, and perhaps even disease.

If you haven't been able to dance for some time, your soul may be restless, unsure of a direction, and unhappy. Furthermore, if your "village" no longer dances, you may have forgotten how.

Yoga, dance, music, and theater are helpful, but only if they also let you listen to your own body wisdom and give you the opportunity to let your soul freely move, sing, and speak the way your body wants to speak.

Here is one way you could tend the garden of your soul with a spiritual practice of dance:

Dance of Restoration

1. Take a deep breath and invite the Divine to hold you.
2. Put on music, sing, or hum along as you move. (Think of singing as dancing on the inside.)
3. Begin by moving your hands, circling and articulating your fingers and wrists. Remember to breathe.
4. Giving attention to each of your body parts, proceed to move your arms, including your elbows and your shoulder joints. How do your arms dance?
5. Move into your shoulders and neck. Undulate, roll, jiggle, and stretch your upper body.
6. Continue, gradually moving down into your torso, hips, thighs, knees, legs, and ankles.
7. Let your feet take you to another place, moving in any direction they want.
8. Are you still breathing or singing?
9. Is there a particular part of you that seems silent, restless, or in pain? Taking a deep breath, honor this place, bringing your hands to it if possible. Let this area offer expression either by minimizing or exaggerating the feelings in this body part.
10. Release your concentration on your body parts and move all of you.
11. Receive the blessing of the wholeness that you have, including areas of challenge, giving thanks for this restorative time.

❖ ❖ ❖

A dance of restoration can take many forms. The key is having the intention to listen to your physicality. You can focus on one body part, move your whole body, or start from any point of entry that you choose; for instance, your feet, your head, or your heart. You can even focus on your spirit as you dance with the energy field around and in you.

I think of Harriet, who came to a weekend workshop with restrictive hip pain. She had taken a plane to get to the workshop, but after arriving, she felt hindered and frustrated. She longed to be able to move freely again. I encouraged her to honor the limits of her body, dancing *within* her limits rather than resisting them. Over the weekend, I observed her warm up. She didn't lift her legs or pivot quickly. She kept her body centered and relaxed. At times, she seemed to be in conversation with her hip, inviting it to tense and relax. The rest of her body was still getting most of the benefit of movement, which promoted greater flexibility and joint freedom, plus increased flow of blood, oxygen, and lymph, all of which helped her hip to heal. The next month when she returned for another weekend workshop, her hip pain was gone. She was certain that continuing to dance with respect to her injury helped her regain her range of motion.

Was Harriet's restoration a form of spiritual healing? When we get injured or feel less physically whole, it directly impacts our spirit. Our power, joy, self-compassion, and freedom are all affected. Some people hate their bodies for betraying them. When we lose capacity, we're forced to revise our identity. The resentment, grief, and frustration of losing what we used to do can cripple our spirit just as much as it can impinge on our movement.

Even people who have beautiful bodies, perfect coordination, and "no problems" may suffer from low self-esteem. The dance of restoration is an opportunity to express gratitude for our bodyspirit.

This happened in an intergenerational, multicultural session where Soyinka led five adults and five children in a warm-up very much like the dance of restoration. We squirmed and delighted in moving each body part. There was a mom who had lost her hair due to chemo for breast cancer; her two creative, homeschooled kids; a grandma in her seventies who loves to dance; her shy grandkids, a two-year-old boy, carrying a toy truck, and his sister. There was also a single mom whose first-grade daughter wrapped herself around her mom 70 percent of the time. Everyone was enjoying moving. The little boy, who just wanted to watch, was also made to feel welcome.

Following Soyinka, we reached out our arms and wrapped them around ourselves in a hug. Soyinka said, "Just say to yourself, 'I love you. I love. I love you.' Like a chant." As I did this, I watched the moms with their eyes closed, swaying and saying those words. They seemed to know that this was important work. As a mother myself, I didn't have to imagine how important.

We moved and played as a group for an hour and a half. By the end, the littlest and shyest boy was dancing, asking people to talk in funny voices, and blowing bubbles. I thought to myself, "Love your neighbor as yourself" is the golden rule. How lucky that in that session we got to do both.

STRESS: "EXFORMATIONAL" DANCING

Stress is an everyday affair. Challenges hit us from all angles. The truth is, we are sponges absorbing the world around us. Science has proven this. Scientists know exactly how tiny mirror neurons create empathy and make us receptive to the big and little versions of love, joy, grief, rage, and the subtle desperation of others. All of us who are "tuned in" to the world around us experience information overload at some point. To cope, we learn to moderate our sensitivity or the "stuff" sneaks up on us until we get "full of it."

It's easy to unconsciously treat our bodies like trash compactors, cramming more and more information in, only to wonder later why we feel so heavy and burdened. Living in the information age, receiving constant images, connections, and experiences at an addictively insane rate, makes me wonder: What if over 80 percent of the "stuff" we deal with on a body level isn't really "ours"? I have no scientific data about that other than hearing hundreds of people testify to feeling 80 percent better after dancing and breathing to clear their space.

People interested in health already know how much it helps to reduce stress when they work out, take bike rides, go on walks, paint, breathe deeply, garden, or pray. Without these regular, joyful practices, the events of any given day can make even a saint feel crabby. As people of the twenty-first century, we need regular ways to cleanse our bodyspirits more than ever. And why shouldn't this be fun?

My colleague, Phil, coined the term *exformation* as the opposite of *information*. We needed a word to describe our experience of dancing to move out unwanted information. More descriptive than the idea of "expressing" ourselves, *exformation* recognizes the accumulated experiences that collect bit by bit in an endless stream of data, coming at and taking form in our bodies. Exformation is a way of sending all that information back out. Exformation takes seriously that both superfluous and pertinent information "matters" on the body level. If you don't think so, consider the growth of "media fasting"—retreats, spas, and meditation in response to managing all the incoming data.

Exformation is more than releasing emotion; it is communication. Exformation recognizes our need for real physical forms to help us move information out—or at least up to a level of consciousness. Any physical activity we do in a repetitive, soothing, or vigorous pattern can qualify as exformative. This is why going for a walk can be a good way to let our ideas surface and help us think things over. What physical forms help you move things out? Is it doing the dishes or mowing the lawn? Rocking or sitting on a porch swing? Singing in a choir? Journaling? Painting? Salsa dancing? These actions probably help you relax and sort out the barrage of data you've internalized.

Exformation also validates that our bodies are designed to react. Watch children. They instinctively express reactions to people, places, and things. Inhibiting some of these reactions is important as we age, but it doesn't take away the fact that the body continues to be fundamentally involved, reacting to every situation. The more challenging the situation, the more our body needs outlets, either in the moment or at some future point. Exformational dancing allows for safe, nonverbal, nonrational forms for communicating reactive buildup that we need to release.

As a mother, a wife, a leader in my community, a caregiver, and a responsible citizen, I do not want to get shut down, feel overwhelmed, or turn to self-medicating to deal with stress and reaction. I need to exform regularly. I don't have to say a word or burden others; I just have to move and breathe. The beauty of this is that in seasons of frustration or anger, powerlessness or pressure, my movement practice is in place to help me deal with them.

On one occasion when my child was hurt by someone, it pained me deeply, but I needed to stay present for her. I went into action, finding the resources needed to deal with the trauma. I was proud that I remained calm and focused, since there had been times when my stress erupted in unhealthy ways, adding to the turmoil. But not this time. Yet as days passed, although my body felt calm, my head buzzed with a cloud of anxiety. The chemicals cortisol and adrenaline, which my brain had released in the presence of danger, were still switched on and flowing. The only way to switch off this chemically induced anxiety was to complete the cycle of emotional communication about this event.

Fortunately, I knew to go to the studio with a friend and dance. I set up a series of three uninterrupted exformational dances. More than catharsis, I believe that the sacred art of dance, helped by a witness, honored my motherly stress and moved it to a place outside my body. At the end of the dance, in silence, I bowed and finished my ritual of exformation.

A simple way to practice exformational dancing is with jerky and smooth movements. Try this one-minute dance to release accumulated stress:

Dance of Exformation

To warm up:

~ For ten seconds, make jerky movements.
~ For another ten seconds, make jerky and *slow* movements.
~ For ten seconds, make *smooth* movements.
~ For another ten seconds, make smooth and *fast* movements.
~ Then, combine smooth and jerky moves any way you want, imagining anything that has "jerked you around" or that you'd like to "smooth out."
~ If jerky movements are enlivening, do more of them. Even if you're required to hold your energy back at work, at school, or at home, you don't have to now.
~ If the jerky movements challenge you, take them as a confession, a brief way to own the complex dynamics you hold.
~ Now play some music as you dance to exform.
~ When the dance is over, take a deep breath. Notice if there is more to move out. If so, continue.
~ When you are ready, rest in stillness. You may want to journal to reflect.

❖ ❖ ❖

Sometimes it's enough to do a minute-long dance to release the jerky parts of life and smooth things out again. Other times, your body may present you with a truth that you can't avoid. Doing a dance of exformation can help you tune into a feeling, memory, or difficult relationship that calls for more attention.

When our perceptions of how things "oughta be" doesn't match what's happening, we often feel it in our bodies as stress. When something creates enough bodily pain or irritation, it can be a relief to let the truth be known, at least to ourselves. The word *confess* means to tell the truth, and a brief dance to confess your humanity to God can restore balance. In a dance of confession, you can move any truth to God, including hurts, resentments, and doubts.

Dance of Confession

1. Begin with music or in silence.
2. Take several deep breaths, offering this dance to God.
3. Let your body take a shape. The shape doesn't have to be expressive of anything in particular.
4. Make another shape, then another.
5. Move quickly from shape to shape and then slowly. Sense the transitions as well as the stopping places.
6. Let the stillness in each shape fill with awareness.
7. Allow yourself to be in whatever "shape you're in": tense, soft, big, little, demanding, pushy, pliant, weak.
8. If you want, allow your body to move with more feeling, expressing what is in you.
9. Bring the dance to a close with a gesture of reassurance or offering. You can give yourself a hug, or you could bow or surrender in a prostration. Give the truth of your body over to the love of God.
10. Afterwards, take time to journal anything you notice. Especially if you don't have the benefit of a witness, writing can complete the experience of telling the truth. Are there words for your sensations, feelings, or thoughts? What words of reassurance from God come to you?

❖ ❖ ❖

"SHADOW" DANCING

I am not considered a depressed person. If anything, I'm too upbeat, humor-filled, and energetic. However, having a career of natural "antidepressants"—dance, play, art, community building, and theology—did not prevent me from a midlife dropoff into the abyss. Depression is both a disease caused by a chemical imbalance in the brain and a physical symptom of life's difficulty. Today, I am grateful that depression taught me to dance with what I call "the dark side of the moon," a place beyond even shadows. I learned to be more welcoming of darkness as part of who I am.

In an article titled "The Startling Truth about Your Own Dark Side," writer Aimee Carter described entering her darkness, which she identifies as "my own shadow":

> Today there is a breezeway into my own shadow. The night dark velvet curtains part easily when I choose to visit there, and the candle I bring to the wounded parts of myself that I haven't had time to care for is welcome and well known. Instead of being a neglected and dusty vault, it is a useful and supportive envelope of nurturing protective energy. Most of my old wounds have been transformed into gleaming tools and powerful antidotes that I now know how to wield and administer to both myself and others.

Shadows are interesting phenomena. As a kid, I wanted my mom to leave the door to my room open at night, as much for security as for the light show it allowed on my bedroom wall. I could raise my hand and make shapes that became animals, appearing, disappearing, and transforming at will.

When was the last time you considered your physical shadow? You can begin befriending the idea of shadow as part of your life by including it in a movement meditation.

Shadow Dance

~ Raise a hand and find your shadow. Notice its shades and shapes.

~ Follow your moving hand. As your hand rises, the shadow might get larger and more ethereal. As it comes down close to the surface of the floor, table, or wall, it may focus and darken.

~ Play around, making weird shapes with your shadow. It's not important to make them into something, unless you can't resist doing so.

~ Dancing with your shadow, notice your shadow as a faithful accomplice and yet not exactly you.

❖ ❖ ❖

Casting a shadow is physically unavoidable. Yet when it comes to our "emotional or moral shadows"—anything deemed opposite of our lighter, loving selves; anything too emotional, weird, or dangerous—we do everything in our power to hide them. Those who value love and joy are often shocked by their feelings of hate, doubt, or rage.

What really saddens me is how easily the light side morphs into the dark side. Sometimes our light, joy, vulnerability, laughter, and innocence become the shadow, and we feel as if it's necessary to keep them hidden. I'm also grieved at how easy it is to become complicit with the collective shadow. No matter how hard we try, we are connected to the evil shadows of racism, greed, and war.

When I was the pastor of a church, I tried to practice nonviolence, but I was well aware that most members of my congregation had jobs making weaponry for the defense industry. Their paychecks constituted my earnings. Is it any surprise that, praying before I was hired, I envisioned a long, flat road only to see a nuclear bomb explode at the end of it? Was this my path? Yes. Most religious leaders come to know their communities as a source of big-time shadow work.

Just as we cannot escape our physical shadow, we must learn to dance with the complexities of our emotional shadow. The harder we try to be good, the more evident our "badness" becomes. If we're clueless about our shadow, others seem more than able to see and name it for us. "You are so lazy, such a workaholic, so quiet, so loud, so nosey, so, so, so ..." How do they know? We're doing everything we can to lock these truths up and out of sight. The truth is, if we can't befriend and integrate our shadows, our dark sides rise up in ways over which we have no say. Prior to my breakdown, I tried to ignore my underlying fatigue and desperation as I demanded to make it all "okay." But my shadow grew and grew until my soul cried out. I didn't realize how hard I was working and working to keep the world in balance—so much so that I was playing God. One night I found myself crying, and I couldn't stop. Suddenly, I just wanted to die. I had lost all energy. Everything ached. The next day I went to the doctor. My depression had reached a crisis point.

In *Spirituality and the Healthy Mind: Science, Therapy, and the Need for Personal Meaning*, Mark Galante, professor of psychiatry and director of the Division of Alcoholism and Substance Abuse at New York University Medical Center, suggests that traditional psychiatry deals with symptoms and conditions through medication, yet doesn't address the issues of meaning in life that often underlie conditions like depression. In psychiatric texts, the spiritual basis underlying depression is rarely mentioned.

If we don't have ways to imbue shadowy experiences with meaning, we end up in positions where they can intensify and control us. Stories of good and evil in sacred texts, fairy tales, movies, and art help us communicate with the shadow. Think of Edvard Munch's painting "The Scream." Munch's impressionist image is found on T-shirts and mugs today and even has us laughing as we acknowledge reactions to the human shadow. Horror movies freak us out, but we pay money to go see them so we can laugh at our own reactions.

The shadow side of meaning relates to the spiritual sense of morality and immorality, as well as more difficult questions about our relationship with God. Religions remind us that evil, the devil, or whatever you might call it, lurks just beyond the throw of the light. If we cannot unmask our potential for dancing with the devil, we arm the dark with greater strength.

In his book *Shadow Dance: Liberating the Power and Creativity of Your Dark Side*, psychotherapist David Richo writes that our limitations are, "paradoxically, the very and only stuff of wholeness," and he poses the challenge, "Do you dare to love what you have hated all your life?" He suggests that every "negative" characteristic equally encompasses its positive side, and he offers a list of eighty-two contrasting emotional qualities. In one column are what he calls "negative shadows" ("What we see in others, but do not see in ourselves"), and the facing column shows the contrasting "positive shadows" ("the kernel of lively energy we have in us potentially, but do not see"). Here is a sampling of some of these contrasting qualities:

Addictiveness	Steadfastness
Anxiety	Excitement
Arrogance	Self-confidence
Caretaking	Compassion
Defensiveness	Preparedness
Fear	Caution and vulnerability
Hate	Healthy anger
Helplessness	Openness to support
Impatience	Eagerness
Impulsivity	Spontaneity
Laziness	Relaxedness
Perfectionism	Commitment to doing things well

The words themselves are physically suggestive. If we play with the movement qualities they evoke, we can release stalled energy. I often find that the etymology of a word gives me movement clues. *Steadfast*, for instance, comes from the Middle English *steed*, meaning "place," and *faste*, meaning "fast." I get an image of moving fast in one place. As I physically enact this, inner light bulbs go on. As a person who is considered steadfast, playing with dancing fast in one place gives me ideas about my "stick-to-itiveness," what one friend calls my "attention intensity disorder." As I dance with this, I gather clues about the shadow side of steadfastness—addictiveness. It helps me release old ideas that hold me back, allowing me to more compassionately embrace the strengths and liabilities of being mercilessly and mercifully faithful.

What if emotions are actually movement? What if resisting "e-motion" is to resist healing itself? Some healers suggest that our bodies are designed to move emotional energy in the most efficient way possible. If we are anxious, for example, shaking and quaking can be helpful. If we are angry, then muscular thrusting is a natural release. If we are fearful, then breathing keeps us from becoming overly rigid. If we feel love, then our flowing, free, open movements distribute these energies throughout our bodies and out into the world.

If you have ever been in a drama class, you may remember the revelation of meeting your shadow side in an exercise. I'll never forget the day my friend Susan faced me from the other side of the studio. Our company wanted to incorporate more emotional gray tones and vibrant, wilder energies in our performances. The assignment was this: "From opposite sides of the room, give your partner a short movement and voice phrase that reflects their 'evil twin.'" Susan knew me well. She took one look at me and with her best rendition of an exasperated, hangdog physicality, swaggered into the space and said, "I don't give a rat's ass."

I was supposed to repeat her movement and words, matching her bodily interpretation of my shadow. Instead, I burst out laughing. She had nailed me on a truth that I resist. I laughed and laughed until I was on the floor, hysterical, my enlightened shadow taking me to my knees. Susan knew that "I don't give a rat's ass" is something I would *never* say, as the queen of caring about everything, but there it was in full view: *"I don't give a rat's ass."* Years later, surrounded by playful rat sculptures and images, I am reminded that I do—and don't—need to care about everything.

Our shadows often stem from repressing emotions. Over my piano is a small collection of masks from Africa, Asia, and Latin America. None are "pretty," but I like them because, frankly, I'm jealous that masked dancers get to wear fear, anger, and lust on their faces as they forage for fruit in humanity's shadow lands.

A mask can be a kind of creative "confessional" for emotions. Rather than analyzing our shadow, if we play with our shadow side in creative tasks, we can more easily light the way for aspects of shadow to emerge before they take us down. Dancing with your "evil twin" playfully releases repressed energy and can help you enjoy the natural aspects of human wholeness.

Masked Dances

1. Hold your face in a frozen position, then moosh it around.
2. Squirm your mouth into a weird shape.
3. Let your body mold into a "mask" to match the expression on your face.
4. Taking a few steps in any direction, move your body with the energy and feeling of the mask.
5. Take a deep breath and shake out the mask.
6. Let your face assume another "mask." Exaggerate it as much as possible.
7. Mold your body into the shape of this mask, and move with that dynamic.

8. Add a little wiggling of your hips, even though it may not match the character of the mask.
9. Add a little dance, shaking a pointer finger at the world.
10. Relax this mask, take a deep breath, and let it out with a sigh.
11. "Put on" one more mask. Exaggerate it, as you mold your body to match and move.
12. Speak a repetitive syllable or sound to accompany your movement.
13. To end, take some deep breaths and shake everything out.
14. Take some time to journal and notice anything about these masked parts of you. What or who do they remind you of? Did you enjoy or resist the idea of playing with your masks? Either way is fine.

❖ ❖ ❖

We don't have to become our shadows, but if we invite them out and play with them, they're less likely to hide in the balcony and take potshots at us when we're not looking. More importantly, shadow dancing can be liberating. Besides giving us much-needed laughs, we're less likely to erupt in anger when we confront the shadows of other people. Wise people call this "doing your work."

There is no better way to be introduced to your spiritual shadow than through silliness. It may feel corny, but in the spirit of grace, creativity, and fun-loving, if you let yourself be transformed by the alchemy of a new behavior, you'll unleash all the pressure it took to hold yourself back. If you let go of the worry about "dancing well," you will get an energy boost and a dose of integration. And you'll get clued into some mysterious, ridiculous, and often heartbreakingly beautiful truths.

What are some things you're not supposed to do? Turn a few of these behaviors into ten-second spiritual "No-No!"

dances. The Divine knows and accepts you any way you are, so why not give a few of these a try?

No-No! Dances

- ~ "You should be peaceful." No-No! Do a ten-second ranting dance. Stomp around and punch the air.
- ~ "You should be sober." No-No! Do a drunken, blurry, flop-and-drop-dead dance.
- ~ "You should be prim and proper." No-No! Dance for ten seconds with your butt sticking out.
- ~ "You should be reserved!" No-No! Shake parts that you shouldn't shake.
- ~ "You should be demure!" No-No! Dance sassy, hands on your hips or thrusting your pelvis.

❖ ❖ ❖

If playing with things that you have been told not to gives you energy and doesn't hurt others, you could push your boundaries a little further and reclaim honest-to-God parts of your joy and light. Going beyond intellectual safety, when we experiment on a body level using creative acts, we may get reputations for being "interesting, exploratory, and a little nuts," but we are far more likely to heal from the unnecessary shouldn'ts and don'ts that clutter most people's lives. Dancing with your shadow includes taking things you normally joke about more seriously. Here are a few examples to show what I mean. You could:

- ~ Find a piece of cloth in a color you've refused to wear and dance with it.
- ~ Mimic a dance form for which you have no talent. Don't make a joke out of it. Savor your sensations.
- ~ Reverently dance your feeling for a gender other than your own.
- ~ Dance in the mud. Get down and dirty and rejoice in the earth.

Trauma: Dancing for Soul Retrieval

A friend moved to Asia for her husband's work and went through a lengthy process of grief, deeply missing the nourishment of her community. Depleted, she mourned, "I miss the days when I had boundless energy and felt that I had much to offer friends and students. I miss being able to openly love. Sometimes I lie awake anxious about our unknown future. I cry and mourn my losses in those wee hours, wanting some of what used to be, friends who understand and can hug me tightly. I miss unashamed laughing and crying body to body. I've learned the body of a closed person. I long for joy, contentment, a sense of well-being, but I fear they're gone, something of my past, packed away like all the things I long to hold." My friend didn't recognize who she'd become, and neither did I.

Most of us encounter this kind of loss at some time in our lives. When we suffer accidents, deaths of friends or loved ones, injuries, or abuses, life can feel profoundly unsafe. Parts of us are likely to "give up" on staying present and move off to a hidden place. Our body offers this solution in graciousness. Unable to integrate trauma, our vulnerable parts, such as our confidence or calm, depart and leave a gaping hole.

When we experience overwhelming grief, violence, or shock, it is common to lose heart, lose our mind, and lose basic parts of our soul. We get psychically winded as life's abruptness knocks more than breath out of our body. People tell stories of feeling suspended outside or above their body. Psychology calls this experience "disassociation." When it feels permanent, healers call it soul loss.

Soul loss, an extreme defense mechanism of our bodyspirit, is a form of self-protection that freezes, contracts, or removes entire parts of consciousness in ways that even therapists struggle to help. Loss of energy, focus, passion, joy—and the classic feeling of a hole in our chest—are common indicators of soul loss. In these situations it is too difficult for us to operate as our own healer *and* make ourselves feel safe. Much like surgery, soul retrieval requires therapeutic levels of wisdom and support from those familiar with the language and communication patterns of the soul: imagination, imagery, and myth. Jungian therapists know this is where soul conversations take place.

In *Soul Retrieval: Mending the Fragmented Self*, Sandra Ingerman tells us that "in shamanic cultures people who suffered traumas were given a soul retrieval within three days after a trauma occurred." The healer would pray through dance, sound, and drumming and would journey into the spiritual realms in search of the person's lost part. Accepting the imaginal realm as real, the healer was often able to find and negotiate a reunion with the personas that were hiding.

The word *shamanic* doesn't actually refer to a person or belief system but to the practice of communicating with the spirit world. *Shaman* comes from the Tungus root *ša*, meaning "to know." True healers need to know the soul, understand the way the imagination works, have ethical and consistent practices, and know themselves. Those with healing knowledge respect movement's role in recovery processes. Movement directs both healers and clients to inner authority and acts like a "healing water gushing up to eternal life."

Anthropologist Angeles Arrien found that, around the world, indigenous healers often asked suffering people, "When did you stop dancing? When did you stop telling your story? When did you stop singing your song? When did you lose your ability to simply be on the earth with joy?" The disappearance of these behaviors, once so integral to everyday community life, would have made it easier to diagnose the situation that caused the soul loss. The trauma would have been close to a time when the afflicted person lost her desire to sing, dance, talk, rest, or offer physical intimacy. Once the situation was clarified, the healer could facilitate a ritualized reunion of body and soul, using the elements of movement, shaking, rhythmic incantations, chant, word, image, air, breath, fire, and aroma. Working their imaginal muscles into trance states, they could set about reinvigorating the hurting person's appetite for moving, singing, and wholeness.

Today, even with all our science and medicine, other modes of healing don't replace imagination and dance as healing processes. Though we might not have access to a shaman in our contemporary society, some people have developed similar skillfulness and shamanlike bodies of knowledge.

At the Trauma Center in Boston, expressive art therapists work with the idea that "people need a physical experience that directly contradicts the helplessness and sense of defeat associated with the trauma." Founder and director Dr. Bessel van der Kolk suggests, "Imagining new possibilities, not merely repetitively retelling the tragic past, is the essence of post-traumatic therapy."

Susan's story appeared in the *Oakland Tribune* in an article titled "Trauma Survivors Change Lives through a Dance Revolution." Hit by a car, she endured numerous operations before she joined a dance therapy program. Even though she had steel rods in her body, dancing for her was transformative. She said, "I didn't know I could do this. I can dance. My fear has turned into movement." She regained her feeling of joy and confidence in her body in spite of the outcome of her accident.

In written correspondence, movement therapist Betsey Beckman spoke about creativity in spiritual direction and the powerful role of the guide:

> Creative modalities can be deep enough to speak the truth in symbolic and artistic ways, but the next step is for those expressions to be received and honored. When the truth is received within the therapeutic-spiritual direction relationship, the possibility of right relationship with the other and with God can begin to grow. The therapist or spiritual director can model and embody the possibility of

a God who cares enough to be present to the healing journey in a world which includes deep human suffering. Through this process, as a sense of well being and energetic flow are restored within the survivor, possibilities of connection, soul, receptivity, relationship and spirit open.

You cannot perform a soul retrieval on yourself. In my own experience I wouldn't have the wholeness I have without the knowledgeable support of trained and indigenous healers who helped retrieve parts of me that were lost. Watching them dance on my behalf, I experienced immediate physical shifts. I felt their surpluses of objectivity, energy, and lightness. What a relief when they focused on my needs for a short time. These dancers were like angels.

Just as we don't perform surgeries or organ transplants on our own bodies, recovering lost pieces of our soul requires support. Someone in extreme distress needs an assistant, a guide committed to maintaining her own soul strength, someone who can call on the Divine and fearlessly intervene in imaginal realms. The soul-retrieval process requires training and dedication to the healing process. A good guide is committed to helping a survivor prepare in advance as well as follow up afterwards.

While we may not have the training to be able to offer soul retrievals, we can do one thing communities have always done for those who are traumatized: We can dance on their behalf. Just as we would if someone were hospitalized, by dancing on behalf of a person's wholeness, we can imagine and communicate our hope and confidence for healing. We can pray for her and embody the wholeness that we want for her.

Part of the mystery of prayer is knowing that we are powerless and that, as dancers, we seek intervention from a greater source. When we dance on someone else's behalf, one gift we give is our faith, offered in a dance with love. This does not require great dancing or great dances. Our role is not to try to heal the person or to heap his concerns on our shoulders. Our act of dancing on someone else's behalf is an act of giving him over to the care of God. When I do this, I imagine my pictures of concern creased into the focused place between my eyes. Releasing them up in the air, I take a deep breath and shake out attempts to understand or help. My only job is to dance for him and myself, to take care, to enjoy myself, and to place him in God's hands.

I was initially surprised at people's willingness to dance on behalf of others. Ironically, many find it easier to dance for others than for themselves. In a large assembly I attended, worship planners had fashioned a service that gave people simultaneous access to multiple forms of prayer. Children and adults offered spoken prayers into a microphone. People lit candles. Some sang songs. Musicians played on instruments. Healing stations offered "laying on of hands." Dancers offered movement prayers onstage; thirty or more of us danced on behalf of the collective concerns as they were voiced. The spirit in the room was palpable. This group of normally rational religious folk hardly recognized themselves. Afterwards, many said that it was the most powerful experience of prayer they'd ever had.

I invite you to give this movement form of intercessory prayer a try.

Dancing on Behalf Of ...

1. Bring a person to mind for whom you feel concern.
2. Take a deep breath and release the need to personally intervene or heal her pain.
3. If need be, shake out your own concerns. Put your fingers on the focused place between your eyes, and toss your own worries up in the air.
4. Using prayerful music, such as keyboard or flute, or even something upbeat, imagine something you like about her.

5. Imagine blessing her with your hands. Gestures of blessing may lead to shapes, as embodied prayers. Or you may sense the kind of energy and dynamic that you see missing in her and dance it as a portent of things to come.

6. As you dance for her, you may be surprised at movements that come. Gracious communications will arise. I have never seen it fail.

7. Now go one step further. As you move, let this dance serve you, too. Connecting to your own desires can also bless you with wise, intuitive, healthy results. This might seem paradoxical. "Can a prayer on behalf of someone else also benefit me?" On a body level, yes, it does. The biblical command to love your neighbor as yourself is not theoretical; it is how the body works best.

CHAPTER SIX

DANCING FOR SPIRITUAL DIRECTION

"One Simchat Torah evening, the Baal Shem himself danced together with his congregation. He took the scroll of the Torah in his hand and danced with it. Then he laid the scroll aside and danced without it. At this moment one of his disciples who was intimately acquainted with his gesture, said to his companions: 'Now our master has laid aside the visible dimensional teachings, and has taken the spiritual teachings unto himself.'"

—*Martin Buber*

Almost every aspect of spiritual life can be practiced through dancing. In previous chapters we have explored dance to invoke the Divine, dance for meditation and contemplation, and dance for blessing and healing. Down through time, as people have instinctively danced to align body, mind, heart, and spirit, they have developed dances for different religious needs.

In my teaching on the wisdom of the body at the Pacific School of Religion, I have investigated dance as prayer, as theology (theokinetics), as social action, for cultural diversity, ethics, proclamation, spiritual direction, community development, healing, biblical study, and in death and dying. My students and I found dance to be relevant to every aspect of human endeavor because our body is central to every part of life. We cannot divorce it, no matter how hard we try.

Joyfully, given the right conditions, dancing is one of the best spiritual directors around. With the support of God, and occasionally a sacred witness, we can enjoy dancing spiritual disciplines, dancing with sacred texts, dancing for discernment, and dancing to discern purpose. But, first, I want to introduce the idea of the "sacred witness." The sacred witness is a key element to dancing as a spiritual practice.

THE SACRED WITNESS

If you find it hard to dance on your own, you are not alone—especially when it comes to dancing your soul. People in classes and workshops repeatedly ask me, "Why don't I do this at home?" Truthfully, I don't know. I only observe that dancing alone is hardly the norm. A seventy-year-old dancing healer once said to me, "I can turn and jump and roll around alone in my studio, but little happens. A loving witness makes a huge difference." Witnesses play a crucial role in the spiritual discipline of dance. Witnesses do more than "just watch."

Dancing our body wisdom is powerful and wild. Even one other person can provide security should we unlatch our psyche and let our spirit fly. This is why we need therapists, priests, and shamans. If we could have "burning bush" direct encounters with God alone, why wouldn't we? I think people find dancing more akin to Moses's experience of finding God in a burning bush than safely reading about it.

Witnesses create a secure base. They literally hold still in a spot and give the dancer their steady attention. This grounding empowers the dancer's sense that someone is looking out for him, caring enough to let him delve into deeper waters. The part of the dancer that usually has the job of staying aware of the surroundings can relax.

Witnessing is not absentminded gazing; it reincorporates visual attention alongside all the other senses. Ordinarily, we may tend to home in on a particular subject and give it a good hard look. Our tightened focus echoes throughout our body. Muscles in our neck, back, butt, and heart follow suit until we are no longer aware of sensations other than those in our head. Witnesses, instead of operating with visual-analytical tunnel vision, broaden the view to the big picture. They take in what they see and feel. It is not a matter of being an intrusive voyeur, but of being prepared to be moved. Easy focus allows witnesses to see *and* to perceive things via other senses as well.

In Old English, the word *witness* means "to know." To know and be known is a description for intimacy. In Hebrew the word for *knowing* refers to sexual intimacy. Knowing is bodily. It is whole. Like a good listener, a sacred witness "knows with" the dancer. At a level deeper than words, dancer and witness share a body-to-body phenomenon where the witness feels the mover's movement in her own body. When she is done dancing, a witness gives the dancer time to collect herself and notice the experience. When the dancer is ready to receive comments, the witness practices sharing specifically what was moving and enjoyable. When there are no words that can express the experience, the witness infuses confidence into the stillness as the sharing unfolds. Sacredness multiplies in the body of the witness, in the space between them, and in the unseeable contact with the One in Whom We Dance.

Attending a Cochiti Indian corn dance in New Mexico, I entered a plaza where hundreds of dancers, attired in sacred garments, moved in spokes. People sat in lawn chairs around the perimeter of the dancing circle. The reverence was palpable. For me, as a white woman starved for this kind of community, the experience felt surreal, like a dream.

An elder in front of me turned to a few chatty tourists and said, "Shhhhhhhhhhh." Clearly, this dance was prayer. Those who witnessed were part of it.

One man then quietly asked another, "Not dancing?"

"Not this time" was the reply. Apparently, members of the village had a say about when they danced or witnessed. Both were necessary.

Sacred witnesses can "know with" but need not "know-it-all." Since the mystery of each bodyspirit is as unfathomable as God, witnesses are not required to answer questions, heal a person, or *do* anything at all. In fact, the less they try to do, the better. They are a partner to Mystery.

Two women I know meet weekly to move and witness each other. When one woman went away to do training, they kept the practice going. Each one danced before a video camera and sent it to the other. They developed such faith in the ability of the other to hold space for her that they could even dance and witness each other virtually.

In this age of anonymity, to have someone offer his loving presence to us is a tonic. Sacred witnesses are precious. When someone offers us ease, neutrality, appreciation, and the willingness to be moved by us, we gain an "outside eye" for our soul work. This transformative gift is one you and I can give with simple presence; "showing up" for each other in this way provides much more.

WITNESSES FORM "RITUAL CONTAINERS"

Witness and dancer, through their designated roles, set up a sacred partnership. This creates a unique space for spiritual practice. By simply determining a beginning and end to our time, we establish a "ritual container." The middle, whether ten minutes or an hour, is where journeys become sacred. The witness stays accountable for what is really happening in space and time and helps a dancer begin, end, and, afterwards, notice what hap-

pened. For the dancer, this may be like being attended by ancestors, saints, spirits, guides, and angels. It can even be lifesaving.

In the Dagara tribe in West Africa, Malidoma Some
explains in *The Healing Wisdom of Africa*, when a person dies, the
body is placed before the group and the singing, dancing, drumming, and wailing ensue. Witnesses attend to those close to the
deceased, keeping them from hurting themselves while they
move the chaotic mourning energy out of their body.

WITNESSES MIRROR NONANXIOUS PRESENCE

Using easy focus, the witness relaxes. This communicates directly
to the mover's body. On some level, this lessens anxiety about
being judged and encourages heart and soul to open further.

In the practice called Authentic Movement, one person
moves in free expression while another observes. As described
beautifully on the Authentic Movement website, "The witness
brings a receptive quality of clear attention to the mover. The
witness is mindful of the inner world of sensation and meaning,
judgment and criticism. Though personal shadow issues may
emerge, the witness accepts the mover without analysis or direction and speaks only when the mover asks for a response. The
mover and witness together can achieve a level of perception of
self and other that evokes deep respect and empathy." Whether
in spiritual companionship or friendship, the gift of ease transfers
grace instantaneously.

WITNESSES "HEAR" WHAT WE HAVE TO "SAY"

The Hopi Indians have a saying, "To watch us dance is to hear
our hearts speak." A witness helps us complete the communication cycle. Once our body has "spoken" to someone, we often feel
as if we can "move on."

I am grateful to all the people who have witnessed me dance.
In seasons of extraordinary stress, death, or psychic disarray,
companions who willingly witnessed my dancing allowed me to

dive into truth without belaboring it. Afterwards, they affirmed and reflected with me, and gave me a chance to grab hold of experiential lessons. They changed my life.

WITNESSES EMPOWER

The back-and-forth interchange of one person making something and another person witnessing it in the spirit of affirmation sets up a creative pulse. The energetic interchange between the mover and the one moved is a rhythm of empowerment. When this empowerment is repeated over and over between individuals and in community, people power rises up. Spirit sings.

Lisa Laing dances with women in a Connecticut prison. She says, "I start by teaching the women how to witness and affirm each other. So few of them have been affirmed or witnessed with love. Many don't even know that it is possible, much less fun. When they begin to feel the rewards of this, it not only changes their relationship to one another, but it also it affects the way they parent and partner. It is a key to life."

WITNESSES CAN ACTIVELY PARTICIPATE WITH US

Physical empathy bonds us. When a person weeps, for example, we may offer him a shoulder or a tissue. Something similar happens when we witness someone dance; we may instinctively feel like moving with him. When this happens, an observer may morph into an "active witness," dancing nearby without interfering, offering visceral companionship. The synchronizing current between dancer and witness can be mysterious and beautiful.

I once saw a man designated as a witness leave his seat at the edge of the space and begin moving behind the dancer with care and attention. He was sometimes close and sometimes at a distance. When he and his partner switched roles, the woman actively witnessed the man. She, too, danced with mirrorlike support and playfulness. She tried on things that he did; she was with him.

Those who take turns in this relationship—sometimes becoming the mover, sometimes the witness—contribute to each other. The spiritual direction and disciplines inherent in both roles are strengthened.

❖ ❖ ❖

I invite you to join with another person taking turns functioning as a sacred witness for each other. If you immediately start thinking, "But I wouldn't know how to do that!" remember this: There is nothing you need to know. Take a deep breath, release your focus, and open up to receive the gift of a dance.

Witnessing a Dance

BOTH WITNESS AND DANCER

1. Decide who will dance first. Choose a short piece of music (three minutes or so).
2. If the dancer has a desire or intention, share it, but don't get bogged down in talking.
3. The witness should sit at the edge of the space or, for the one-arm dance suggested below, at least two arm lengths away in order to be able to take in the whole body of the dancer. (There are obviously many ways the dancer might choose to move. This one-arm dance can be especially helpful if this is the first time witness and dancer have shared this experience.)

WITNESS

1. Take a deep breath; let it out with a sigh. Shake out one arm and then the other and whatever you are "sitting on."
2. Soften your focus, preparing to receive the "good" from the dancer before you.
3. Release your obligation about needing to know where this dance is going.

4. Like witnessing nature or a beloved animal, be curious as you connect to the movement and imagery of the dance.
5. Turn on the music for the dancer.
6. Read the instructions for the one-arm dance below to the dancer as she moves.

DANCER

1. Raise one hand in the air and "dance" each of these movements for ten seconds at a time:
    ~ Let your arm move around through space taking up as much space as you can.
    ~ Move your arm both smooth and fast.
    ~ Now move your arm smooth and slow.
    ~ Move your arm in a jerky way.
    ~ Then move your arm jerky and slow.
    ~ Make a shape with your arm. Make more shapes.
    ~ Bring your hand into contact with your skin. Move to another point of connection.
2. Follow the flow of your hand into a dance. Consider blessing any events or people from your day.
3. When the music ends, come to a rest.

WITNESS AND DANCER

1. Turn off the music.
2. Take a deep breath.
3. Take time for the dancer to notice anything from the dance.
4. When the dancer seems to be finished, the witness shares what she has noticed and what she has received.

❖ ❖ ❖

DANCING SPIRITUAL DISCIPLINES

Wouldn't it be wonderful to be loving, calm, peaceful, patient, cleanly, mindful, organized, charitable, compassionate, money-wise—and why not throw in attractive, funny, talented in arts and sports, and fantastic at public speaking? As an artist, a writer, a mom, and a woman, I've learned that just about everything that I want more of in life is going to require some disciplined, repetitive practice. Rats! My gifts are few; my desires are many. Humility turns out to be one of the easier virtues to acquire. All I have to do is try something new and humility is mine! There is no escaping it. No matter how much I progress, I frequently have to return to practicing behaviors that I thought I had a handle on. My body devolves into old practices. Higher functioning isn't a given, but the result of staying in practice.

Practice is key. As my colleague, Phil, says, "As I understand the science of the brain, as limited as it may be, when we practice a certain behavior, we are creating and then strengthening new neural pathways. If we stop practicing, the pathways will degrade. It isn't enough just to have an idea—we need to find ways to implement it. We may know that it is good for us to floss (or diet or pray or exercise or call our mothers once a week), but only until we find a way to do it regularly does it become part of 'who we are.' Only then does the pattern take hold in our lives."

Sometimes, as martial artists, musicians, craftspeople, teachers, and child-rearing experts know, the best practices develop from little actions that we do over and over until they become second nature. Dancing's utter physicality offers intriguing and enjoyable ways to develop our spirituality in incremental ways. For example, being present, here and now, is something many people seek. What if dancing could help us cultivate it?

Sometimes I become more present by shaking my body down into the earth. Where am I? Looking down, I see two feet side by side, ten toes, size 8. So simple. If I pointed a toe, I could show off. I have orthopedic architecture to die for. Yet, flat on the floor my feet simply *are*. They locate me in space. My feet are here, now. The abstractions of future and past fade. As I lift one foot and then the other, beginning to walk, my soles are the ground of my soul. I wonder: If I kept my focus on them, would I be more honest about where I really stand? Am I "walking humbly with God" (Micah 6:8) right where I am?

Come to think of it, I realize that the connective tissue on the bottom of my feet is inflamed as I walk and dance. Is the connective tissue of my soul inflamed? What is really bothering me?

At a minimum, I need to be mindful of my weight bearing, take it easy in my movements, give myself more cushioning with shoes. Taking note, I put on dance shoes. As I step in time to music, I say to myself with each step, "I'm here. Here. Here." It feels good to dance right in the moment. Like coming back to breathing in meditation, my feet remind me where I am again and again.

You can use any anchor point in your body to become more present. If you think of this as a chance to dance and less like spiritual work, you might set the stage for doing it many times. Remember: Most bodies are attracted to fun and joy. As in any practice, repeating this on a regular basis will increase your ability to be grounded in the present moment and help you when being present feels hard.

Dancing to Be Present

1. Put on music that you enjoy as you focus on a body part that grounds you in the here and now—feet, hands, belly, legs, heart?
2. If it helps to anchor you, bring your hands to this location.
3. Take some deep breaths and visually connect with this place; then move your awareness from there to include the rest of your body.
4. Moving, affirm with each breath, "I am here. Here. Here."

5. Continue connecting with each movement, stepping in rhythm, saying, "Now. Now. Now."
6. Grounded in present time, dance. Enjoy being here, now, releasing all concern about these words.
7. When you complete this practice, notice how you feel. If this felt forced, you might need to do some "exformational" dancing first. (See page 84.)
8. Savor any feelings of coming into present time. Plant these sensations deeply in your heart.

❖ ❖ ❖

It is so easy to forget that the simplest physical practices can be done with spiritual intention. By bringing curiosity, affirmation, and attention to moving our body, we can connect right to our soul. On the other hand, spiritual practices can be sneaky. A spiritual master makes his student wash a wall over and over, to the student's annoyance, until the student discovers that he has learned the motion necessary to efficiently deflect a violent attack. Suddenly he realizes that washing a wall has helped him keep peace. You may need to release your pictures of "spiritual" practice a bit in order to really take advantage of the pervasive role of the body and movement in spiritual direction.

Moving nondominant body parts in an exploratory fashion can illuminate body and soul. Don't let your mind overcomplicate the process. The following movement meditations, paired with some music, can be a dance. If you like, you could choose one practice a week as part of a regular spiritual practice.

Body-Centered Movement Meditations

∼ Want more spine in your decision making, to wobble less? Dance with your spine. Wobble, straighten, stretch, and collapse it. What feels good right now? It's fine to hang down and feel gravity. Your spine still supports you when you are relaxed.

∼ Where do you draw strength from in your body? From your edges, your middle, your heart, your deepest core? Can you initiate and celebrate a dance that moves from the center? What happens if you come from a different source of strength? Is it a relief, an option, too hard?

∼ Want a bigger view? Feel stiff-necked? Dance with your neck and shoulders. Turn your head from side to side until it loosens and moves more easily. What happens when you close your eyes? Is focusing controlling your visioning? What is in your peripheral vision? As you dance, what do you notice?

∼ Feel stuck? Play with your hips. Try hip circles in both directions and some "fake hula." Let your hips move any way they want to. Does this make you laugh?

∼ Need more guts? Breathe out loud while you're moving. Bend your legs, lower your center of gravity, your guts, closer to the earth. Can you let your guts dance?

∼ Want peace? Soften your jaw while dancing. Move it around. Dance with your mouth ajar. Do other places tense up? Explore a dance of tensing and releasing.

∼ Resist stillness or hesitant to make a move? Alternate moving with holding still. How are they in partnership in your life?

∼ Overworking? Need to know how to pace yourself? Move fast, then slow. Can you move faster than the speed of your mind? Slower? Can you regulate your energy, force, and speed? Play with changes of energy and the amount of muscle tension you use.

∼ Out of balance? Want more balance? Balance on two legs, then on one leg, then on the other. Where does balance take you? Play with losing balance and regaining it without hurting yourself. Does feeling centered come easy? Explore passing through center, holding it lightly, or maintaining center.

❖ ❖ ❖

DANCING WITH SACRED TEXTS

Moving in relationship to a scripture is another way to evoke body wisdom. When I taught courses on dance and biblical studies, I had people "exegete" references to the body in the text. Exegesis is simply a means of researching a text to discover its deeper significance. Bible scholars analyze everything about the Holy Book's historical references, literary allusions, and formal characteristics, but many discount—because of a lack of body consciousness and the fact that they are limited to written records—that the physicality in a text can be a place for researching as well. Yet when the body is referenced in a text through action, emotion, posture, or in the etymology of the words of a verse, it is an entry point for spiritual understanding. Artists and performers, such as dancers JoAnne Tucker and Susan Freeman, who wrote *Torah in Motion: Creating Dance Midrash*, are privy to this kind of exegetical action research. JoAnne and Susan call their practice of playing with textual body images "dance midrash" (from the Hebrew word for interpretation) and have dedicated their book to using movement for this spiritual practice.

How does this work? Take the verse from the prophet Isaiah that says, "But they who wait for the LORD shall renew their strength, they shall mount up with wings like eagles, they shall run and not be weary, they shall walk and not faint" (40:31, NOAB). I had students play with this phrase on a physical level. We ran, stopped, and walked before ever hearing the text, in order to understand and notice our own physicality. Playing in and around each other was energizing and fun. Next, I had them listen to the text. As we thought about mounting up with wings, we realized that one way to mount up with wings was to lift each person and carry him for a while. With music, the group created a movement meditation of lifting and "flying" each dancer for a few moments, gently helping him land before taking up another person. Our movement midrash gave us new insight into the role of "waiting" on spiritual support as we allowed the community to lift us.

Delving into the deeper kinesthetic meaning, we can investigate the body in many other sacred texts, liturgies, icons, and prayers. Even one line from a sacred text can become a movement mantra and a means of meditating and spiritual practice. One way to play with a given image is to include its opposite. The full range of meaning of any action requires moving through, beyond, and around it again and again. Movement, by its ever-changing nature, requires us to work with ambiguity and paradox. *Ambiguity* literally means to "move between." I have found this next practice to be a helpful way of exploring this.

Movement Mantras

1. Choose a phrase from a sacred text with a physical reference and repeat it several times. An example would be "Open our hearts."
2. Let your body express the shape or gesture in the phrase.
3. Continue to repeat the phrase like a mantra, if you wish.
4. Next, move into a contrasting shape, contracting or covering your heart.
5. Allow a dance to develop as you move between the two shapes.
6. Be attentive to the transitions that link this spectrum of experience. Transitions are important.
7. Repeat your movement pattern over and over until it becomes a movement mantra. Much like a repetitive counting of beads or the rocking prayers of

Hasidic Jews, repetition of movement can deepen contemplation.

8. Alternatively, you can release concerns about creating replicable patterns and let your movement be more expressive.

9. To end, rest in a closing gesture. Notice it. Savor it. Then let it go.

Here are some movement mantras to give you ideas of how to develop your own mantra practices.

~ "God makes me lie down in green pastures."—Dance while lying down and rising up.

~ "I lift up my eyes."—Dance while focusing up, then changing your focus down, around, nowhere.

~ "I stretch to infinity."—Dance while reaching out and contracting in.

~ "Now I walk in beauty."—Dance while walking, running, and stopping.

❖ ❖ ❖

DANCING FOR DISCERNMENT

Do you have a question or concern? Why not take it to your body? One dear friend regularly writes to her body and lets it "write back." Dancing sets the stage for her dialogue; writing brings her body's wisdom to the fore.

When life, love, and suffering leave you speechless, and you don't know what to do or pray for, movement can bring clarity. Your body can work on your behalf. Your body wants to create. More than to be healed or fixed, changed or altered, your body wants to reach toward health even when life feels tumultuous.

I know a group of women in Seattle who called themselves "The Discernment Group." Some of them crossed national borders and traveled over a hundred miles each month to honor each other's body wisdom. For fifteen years they danced together and offered themselves as witnesses to help each other navigate marital shifts, child raising, and vocational directions. They honed their life purposes, helped each other heal when necessary, deepened their connection to Universal Spirit, and danced, danced, danced.

Use of the term *discernment* arose in the Catholic community among those who sought to enter religious vocation. Today we use it to refer to all questions of import where we need guidance, both spiritual and mundane. When we are having trouble distinguishing one choice from another, it can feel as if everything melds together in a mass of uncertainty. In fact, the word *confusion* itself literally means "to fuse together." To gain clarity, we make lists, talk to people, and try to differentiate among the possibilities. If our choices are equally weighted or the decision we need to make is significantly life changing, clarity may be long in coming. Analyzing them as a way to determine the wisest course is slow, tedious, and maybe impossible. Instead, dancing gives our questions space, room to breathe, and lets our "everythingness" dance. Often, when we hold our questions lightly, answers will make themselves known.

Although I am never quite sure what will emerge when I dance for discernment, I almost always gain some insight. God, spirit, and the results of dancing often surprise me, opening things up. What was locked up in confusion "dis-integrates." My choices get clearer. I start to pay attention to my energy, enthusiasm, and consequences. People who dance for discernment say that dancing is faster than talk therapy, and more fun, too!

Dancing to Clarify

1. Select some music for your dance and find a comfortable place to lie down.
2. Invoke God.
3. Raise one hand in the air and "dance" each of these movements for ten seconds each:

~ Let your arm move around through the space. Take up as much space as you can.

~ Move your arm in a smooth way with fast movements.

~ Now move your arm smoothly and slowly.

~ Move your arm in a jerky way.

~ Move your arm jerky and slow.

~ Make a shape with your arm. Make more shapes.

~ Bring your hand into contact with your skin. Then move to other places of connection.

~ Rest.

4. What question do you want to explore?

5. Playfully bring your fingers to your forehead. Toss your thoughts and worries about it up in the air, allowing your mind to open.

6. Play your music and let your hand dance in an easy relationship to the question.

7. When the music and dance end, write down anything you noticed. "Answers" may come in the form of a thought, an image, a feeling, or a sensation. Something that wasn't even on your mind may enter the picture. Pay attention to whatever comes. If nothing of note happened, that is fine, too. Sometimes "no-thing" is the answer we're given. Your spirit may want to focus on something entirely different than what you thought the question was.

❖ ❖ ❖

When you dance for discernment, a witness can be invaluable. Do you know someone sensitive to her own body wisdom who might sit with you without overdirecting you? Coming together for an hour, you can warm up together and alternate as sacred witnesses. It is also fine if only one person receives attention.

I regularly dance for discernment and witness others. One day Mary was my partner. "How are you today?" I asked her.

Looking expectant, her brow crinkled, she said, "I'm fine."

"Is there anything particular you'd like to play with?"

"I don't know."

I waited for her to say more. After a minute I asked, "Would you like to start with a dance?"

Timid, but excited, she nodded yes.

"Would you like to dance with one hand or move your whole body?"

Standing up, Mary said, "Dance with my whole body."

"Would you like music or silence?"

"Music." She was already using body wisdom as she made each choice.

As Mary rose, I intuitively chose a piece of music that I thought would suit her mood. As she began, I saw something take over. She dropped back to her knees and stayed there. A minute went by before she rose and swept around the room, releasing great swaths of energy. At one point, light from the window hit her face. She looked radiant as she breathed.

Suddenly, she folded over. Stumbling and running, she slowed down and stopped, her arms gathering around her torso. She fell back to her knees. When the music ended, she remained quiet for a time.

When she opened her eyes and looked at me, I asked, "What do you notice?"

"I want to give, but can't."

"What's going on?"

"I started a new job. I was going to lead a project. It was just getting going when I was taken off the project. I couldn't believe it. I kept wondering, was I too much? Not enough? I just want to make a difference."

"I saw that in your dance. You spread your wings, and when your face came into the light, you shone."

She looked at me with teary eyes. In our connection, I asked, "Would you like to dance and really let your wings spread, to give that to yourself?"

"I am tired of getting stopped in my tracks just when I get going."

"That's frustrating."

"Yes, it is. I am tired of it!"

"You have big wings!"

"Yes, I think I do."

We sat for another minute, and then I asked her, "What would you like to create?"

"I just want to stomp around."

"That sounds great!" I responded to her body wisdom.

"Do you need music?"

"No."

Without further ado, Mary stood up and stomped and punched, dancing a dance of exformation. Her voice accompanied her movement. I saw her amusement bubble up, too, as she let her truth be known. Then, suddenly, she was done and sat down, breathless.

I felt like applauding. "That was wonderful!"

She laughed in agreement, "Yes, it was!"

Having cleared away some frustration, she reflected on a frustrating pattern in her life where she just gets going and then has to stop. Frustration kept taking over. She began to realize that even if a project ends, her bodily enthusiasm doesn't have to. The enthusiasm of her spirit wants to dance. Enthusiastic contributions to the world around her are hers alone to enjoy and give. She doesn't have to depend on a job or a role to spread her wings.

"Would you like to dance in honor of your enthusiasm?" I asked.

"Yes."

And that is exactly what she did.

❖ ❖ ❖

Another approach to discernment is to dance with a nagging bodily sensation that may be trying to communicate something or a quality in your body that you want to explore.

Once, struggling to discern my relationship to being an ordained minister, I took my idea about ordination "out of my body." As I imagined holding it before me, my vow took form in my mind's eye as a Gothic cathedral. This was *not* the image of ministry I wanted to be housed in! Then I began to dance. With movements of release, I evicted the heavy architectures of service that I carried and invited a new image to reflect the creative work I do. Between moving and stopping in stillness, I had a vision of a Hawaiian lanai, open and airy, in a balmy, breezy climate. What if my vow to God could be more like heaven on earth? As I danced, I knew that this was to be my covenant with God.

The ability to let movement lead you into imaginary places, through kinesthetic imagination, can open a path of understanding. Is there a place in your body or a thought that is pestering you? Could there be some wisdom that your body wants to share? You can "Dance to Understand" any aspect of your being: your emotions, your thoughts, you at a certain age, your family role, your ancestry. Anything you can imagine, you can probably "draw out" and dance.

Dance to Understand

~ Place your hands on a sensation or body part where you feel concern.

~ Select a piece of music that might support this sensation.

~ Prayerfully, imagine pulling the feeling to the outside of your body.

~ For the duration of the music, in stillness and movement, dance with the image or energy that you have before you, lifting it, relating to it, exploring it.

~ Do images or insights come to mind? Notice any shifts in energy or any new information that comes to mind.

~ Is there anything to release? Transform?

~ What information or insight will you bring back inside you? Gather what you want into your being.

~ After sorting out your understandings, dance where you are now.

~ As you conclude, bless your experience, whatever it is. This dance is part of your spiritual journey.

~ Take time to write about the dance. Was there a highlight? An insight? Something you learned?

❖ ❖ ❖

If you need to make a decision between two choices, it can be helpful to do a dance using your two hands. Put one choice in one hand and the other choice in the other hand, and do a dance of decision making. This dance can also be done with a partner, or you could watch two people dancing hand to hand.

Dance of Decision Making

~ Press your palms together, then pull them apart. Recognize that push and pull are part of decision making.

~ Now, let your two hands flow and come together in random connections. Make different shapes as they connect.

~ Bring your hands back together, palm to palm. Notice the feeling of this simple connection.

~ Begin to open the space between your palms, letting them move apart.

~ Drop your hands, then bring them together again.

~ Imagine one hand holding one choice and the other holding the other choice.

~ Release your focus or worry about the decision.

~ With music or in silence, let the dance evolve any
way it wants to.

~ When you are done, take time to write about, or simply take notice of, your body wisdom.

~ Return to the choices you held in each hand. What
do you notice about the relationship of these two
choices? Do you feel moved toward one or the
other? Has any wisdom offered itself?

❖ ❖ ❖

DANCING TO DISCERN PURPOSE

I was in my forties before I discovered that there is a difference
between life purpose, a call, and my gifts. In spite of feeling that
I had received a call from God to ministry and dance, I felt
strangely restless. I enjoyed my work in the arts and spirituality,
and yet felt unfulfilled. Something deeper cried out for expression. Using my gifts didn't seem to be enough. I didn't want to be
known only as a dancer. I wondered why. If a calling couldn't
satisfy me, what could? I was a mom, a wife, a family member, a
professor. Still, something kept haunting me. I began to ask,
"What am I here to do?"

It's easy to miss our purpose amid duties and tasks, but it's
always there. At a minimum, as D. H. Lawrence said, "The living self has one purpose only: to come into its own fullness of
being, as a tree comes into full blossom, or a bird into spring
beauty, or a tiger into luster." Howard Thurman, a beloved writer
and teacher, describes our purpose as "the dream in the heart."
That's how personal it is. He insisted that it's "no outward thing.
It does not take its rise from the environment in which one
moves or functions. It lives in the inward parts, it is deep within,
where the issues of life and death are ultimately determined."
This kind of depth lives in our body.

Searching for the "dream of my heart," my research led to
experts who differentiate between *gifts* and *purpose*. Purpose usu-

ally requires the use of our gifts. A gift is a talent that comes easily, though it needs to be developed, but talents can feel ordinary to us or even boring. How we use our gifts can either promote or hinder our dream. I think of a friend who was a gifted office manager, but her passion was kids. She quit her accounting job to run a daycare center. For me, I realized that being creative is both what I do and who I am. It's a gift. At the same time, if I create constant change in the world around me, people get preoccupied with my rambunctiousness rather than what I'm dreaming about. I'd rather allow people space and encouragement to express who they are. I found that the verb *foster* guides me toward this open, neutral way of being and still allows me to be who I am. To foster isn't that easy for me, but I love the freedom it creates when I manage to do it.

By paying attention to our gifts, we can discern *how* we want to live our purpose. Beginning with celebrating our gifts, we can begin to discern the kind of actions that embody how we want to be in the world.

Dance to Praise Gifts

This practice can be done either with a partner as a witness or alone. Be aware that it can be easier to celebrate the gifts of others than to celebrate your own gifts. And having a witness help you "see" your gifts can be an eye-opening experience.

~ What do people say you are good at? Either with a partner or on your own, brainstorm a list of what other people say you do well. Even if they tease you about a "gift"—"You're so nosey"; "You're so stubborn"; "You're so organized"—put it on the list.

If you have a partner:

~ First, dance on behalf of gifts you see in your partner, lifting up and affirming them. Don't mime. Feel their strengths in your body and let them move you. Savor your partner's inherent body wisdom.

~ Afterwards, notice those gifts together. Name the gifts you see in your partner, and describe how they inspired your actions and movements.

~ Then trade roles as your partner dances on behalf of your gifts in a similar way. Again, take time to notice the actions and movements and how these energies relate to your gifts.

If you are alone:

~ Imagine someone dancing for you. What gifts would they embody? Try stepping into a witness's shoes for a few minutes and translate what gifts you see into movement.

~ Take time to notice and write down what you experience.

~ Remember that your giftedness might not exemplify your purpose. Are there actions or ways of being that would? Make note of words that intrigue you.

❖ ❖ ❖

Gifts make our bodyspirit shine. This is extremely attractive. People want our gifts and literally call on them. "Yoo-hoo, can you come do this?" "You're good at … cooking, nursing, running, singing, math. I need that."

Gifts lead to calls. And, should the Divine reach out and ask for service, religious people describe this, too, as a "calling," the most profound "yoo-hoo" of all. Still, a call differs from a "dream in our heart" in several ways. Although our Higher Power may have called us, even a spiritual calling may not last a whole lifetime. Yet, a purpose will, even in retirement. Our deepest longings and desires continue moving us to action. A call rooted in purpose is like a fire that does not burn out. It's a source of meaning that our soul yearns to express.

I found this to be true while teaching in India. When a friend "called me" to teach in Mumbai, it made me anxious. The challenges of travel, communication, and culture shock were demanding. In spite of this, using my gifts of dancing and creativity for a greater purpose inspired me more than I imagined was possible. I taught for twenty straight days. Though tired, I was never drained or fatigued. When I returned home, I began preparing for my next trip back.

More than an achievement, role, or job, purpose advances something we value, a dream we fall in love with, yet can't own. In Thurman's inspiring words, "It's a quiet persistence in the heart that enables us to ride out the storms of our churning experiences. It is the exiting whisper moving through the aisles of our spirit answering the monotony of limitless days of dull routine. It is the ever-recurring melody in the midst of the broken harmony and harsh discords of human conflict. It is the touch of significance which highlights the ordinary experience, the common event."

Naming our life purpose is less like writing a mission statement and more like listening for the poetic ring of a Tibetan bell from within. A few well-chosen words can act like gongs that will hit the bell of your body. When they do, your purpose will ring true, and your bodyspirit will say, "*Yes!* That's what I'm about." A good place to start discerning your purpose is to focus on successes and joys. "Yeses" carry evidence of your purpose.

In the following dance, feel free to invite a witness to support you. When trying to unveil a thing so integral to who you are, having a companion's outside eyes is useful.

Yes! Dance

~ Recall a real *Yes* moment in your life when what you were doing felt exactly right.

~ Is there music that you associate with this time? Use this music, or a current choice of music, to celebrate.

~ As you reflect on the memory, dance your *Yes!*

~ Afterwards, notice feelings, qualities, gestures, the amount of space you used, and any connections you made. Where in your body did the *Yes* feel strongest?

~ Share your experience with your witness or write it down. Be on the lookout for words that resonate and ring true. What are the nouns? Action verbs?

❖ ❖ ❖

Thank goodness, I learned that claiming purpose didn't mean I had to get busier. Purposes like making a home or nurturing solitude are as much deep longings as cultivating democracy or saving the wetlands. I once met a woman who unambiguously said, "My purpose is to be beautiful." She wasn't particularly gorgeous. There was no idealism in her words. Being beautiful was simply the fundamental truth her soul strived for. Her clarity of purpose helped me to see her as beautiful. Oddly, I suddenly felt more beautiful, too. All she had to do was embrace her beauty and she had an impact.

Your purpose is your longing. You feel whole, fulfilled, and energized when you think about it, play with it, and embody it. It might not be the easiest thing in the world. In fact, purpose tends to be just out of reach, continuously propelling your curiosity and desire.

To discern between gifts, call, and your heart's desire, you might imagine a nested stack of mixing bowls. The biggest bowl of purpose holds all the others, yet when they're neatly stacked, you can look down and see the inside of the smallest bowl present itself, ready to be filled. The "big bowl" of purpose supports the smaller bowls of gifts and call. They all fit neatly together. Dancing is a powerful way to name your "big bowl" and cook up batches of joy in it.

What is your heart's desire? Dancing may lead you to find clarity of purpose.

Dance of Longing

1. With no musical accompaniment, start with a posture that illustrates your dream of how you long to be in the world. Or, you could take a posture showing the opposite of what you long for. Don't worry if you don't feel much in the moment.
2. Take deep breaths in this posture and listen.
3. Begin to move. Be aware of any resistance.
4. Open to images or physical sensations you might feel.
5. Do any words come to mind as you dance?
6. Bring your movements to an end. Take a minute of stillness to recall parts of the dance that were particularly inspiring.
7. After dancing, share your noticing with a witness or write down your findings.
8. Become attuned to specific words or phrases that ring true. Originating from your bodyspirit, they may be clues to your purpose.

❖ ❖ ❖

Your purpose is applicable to all relations, but there may be specific people, groups, natural wonders, animals, and objects to which you are drawn. Defining "who" you serve, and in what context, is key. One friend is a warm and healing physical therapist and healer (her gift), but she'd rather create a nurturing home for herself and her family (her purpose).

Sometimes purpose is bound up with whom we want to serve. Past calls—jobs, volunteer activities, and roles—may be incongruent with those whom we wish to serve now. Past roles may continue to drain our time, thought, and energy until we release them. Sometimes we are so busy with people from our past that we can't get a moment to reflect on the *whom* of our heart's desire. This is where exformation can be helpful. In dance, you can physically release work or relationships that you want to let go of to help clear space to discern your purpose.

Dance to Exform Prior Calls

Take time to review any calls, roles, or relationships that are over. Is there one that you are ready to exform?

1. Take a deep breath.
2. Shake out one hand, the other, your legs, and your middle.
3. Shake out your voice.
4. Swing and sweep your arms. Imagine clearing your space.
5. With intention, dance to playfully release any completed calls. Send any unfinished business from prior jobs or roles back to whoever called on you in the first place. If you need to, send your unfinished business to God.
6. Bow in gratitude for any opportunities you were given.
7. Reflect in your journal or with a witness on your body wisdom. As you danced this dance of exformation, did you experience shifts? Increases in clarity? What are you discerning now?

❖ ❖ ❖

Whether or not you can ever fully articulate your purpose, you may feel it ring true, like a bell inside of you. And if sometimes you cannot feel it ring, perhaps it is not important to know what your purpose is at that time. You may be doing exactly what is required of you. If you are reading books like this, dancing the sacred, and seeking wisdom, your ongoing spiritual growth and development are purpose enough.

CHAPTER SEVEN

DANCING WITH BELOVED COMMUNITY

*"I have perceived that to be with those I like is
enough,
To stop in company with the rest at evening is
enough.
To be surrounded by beautiful, curious, breathing, laughing flesh is enough....
All things please the soul, but these please the
soul well."*
—Walt Whitman, "I Sing the Body Electric"

Teaching creative movement and voice skills in a Mumbai slum, eight Americans and Australians—myself among them—sat across from two dozen young women in a room that functioned as a fashion and design training center. Sewing machines lined the wall. My nonexistent grasp of Hindi and their weak English threw us on the mercy of a translator and body language. I taught them a few practices found in this book. When I asked if they would like us to dance on their behalf, one woman shyly suggested that we dance on behalf of their slum. The government was threatening to demolish the homes that some of them had lived in for a decade. Though most places had no utilities, these were the only homes these young women knew. No interim places were to be provided; they would be homeless. So it was that in that small space, eight travelers improvised a song and dance to respond to this need.

Afterwards, I asked the women, "And would you give us a blessing?" At the time, I didn't realize that they did not come from the same tribe. Unlike the villages we visited where we were consistently greeted with a communal song and dance, these women didn't have a unifying dance or song. They shrugged. So I asked, instead, if someone would be willing to do a hand-to-hand blessing dance with me. A young Hindi woman timidly scooted forward and offered me her hand. Those in the room watched, suddenly aware that both her hand and mine were hennaed with leaves, swirls, and flowers—the same but different. She reached out first, crossing the invisible divide between our cultures. In a brief dance of no more than twenty or thirty seconds, our two hands danced a gracious, if momentary, blessing. The small, spontaneous motions of our souls said more than a thousand words. All of us in that room seemed to stand on that fragile bridge, crossing distances that normally keep us apart. Cultural reserve and apprehension dissolved in that truly sacred dance.

Dancing forms and strengthens relationships. It creates a playground where we can court each other's spirit and rehearse the best ways to behave in partnership. As our movement mysteriously weaves us together in unforgettable alliances, dancing conveys who we are and whose we are. Dancing together as a spiritual practice can accelerate individual and collective experiences of transcendence. Music and dance can make us fall in love with whole groups of people. Such love is the heartbeat of worship.

In the Apocryphal Acts of John, written a few generations after Jesus's death, the story is told of Jesus gathering the community at the end of the Passover meal. It was the night that he would be arrested, and he asked them to join hands in a circle, dancing and singing "Amen" as he chanted phrases like "Grace dances, dance ye all." While it would have been common for such a meal of remembrance to include singing and dancing at the dawn of the first millennium, this particular circle dance, known as the "Hymn of Jesus," ritualized this community's beloved connection and prepared them for what was to come.

Hoping to rekindle the power of this dance, I created a similar dance—modeled after the original—and paraphrased the hymn. To this day, every time I dance and sing these phrases of Jesus, something happens. As the group circles in a simple pattern, holding hands, swinging them rhythmically into and out of the center on each set of Amens, by the end we're singing "Hallelujah" over and over and dancing in a circle of harmonic blessing.

The joy of movement as a spiritual practice hits its stride when we dance with others. If there are recommended daily requirements for health in individual bodies, I think the same applies to group bodies. If groups don't exercise body and soul, then collective soul may wither. I believe there are simple ways to connect, cocreate, and find freedom and joy when we dance with beloved community.

Dancing Hand-to-Hand Connections

Hands bless, create, anoint, caress, tickle, wrestle, and heal. Yet human-to-human contact has become rare in our fast-moving, technologically sophisticated culture. Encapsulated in our virtual bubbles like little boats, we shove off from our landings to join millions of lonely vessels afloat on the sea of daily life. Captains may wave at one another, but that's about it.

"Stay in touch," a woman implores a friend who is leaving for the airport. A father calls his son who has been "out of touch." When I hit an emotional patch, I feel "touchy." It often helps to slow down and hang out with the dog. I wonder, Am I the pet or is he? We both need the hand-fur contact.

At a meeting, a woman became agitated about the lack of heat in the room. A friend smiled, reached over, and rubbed her back for a minute. Such unexpected contact warmed her. Her face melted.

Human affection is a basic need. A "high five," a pat on the back, or a hug generates health through the amazing neurological "software" in our hands. There is a universal power in touch that healers have claimed for millennia. Handprints have been found on the roof of an Indonesian cave, where it is surmised that the shaman initiates blew paint around their hands to create distinctive symbols of healing power. In ancient India, Australia, and Guatemala, hand power is symbolized by a coiled spiral in the palm of a hand raised in greeting. This symbol, with the addition of a tiny heart at the center of the spiral, is always with me. For my daughter's eighteenth birthday, she requested that we each tattoo it on the top of our spines. Hands and hearts apart, yet together.

Spiritual communities encourage connection through the sacred arts of anointing, healing, and blessing. New Zealand Maori men and women rub noses to greet and bring strangers and friends close enough to foster affection and disarm animosity. Thai Buddhists offer massage on temple grounds to encourage priests to receive regular healthy touch. Christian worshippers embrace each other, saying, "Peace be with you." The Dances of Universal Peace, founded by Samuel Lewis, invite people to join hands and hold onto each other's waists.

Contact, however, also brings up cultural questions of safety and trust. Abuse has taught us to keep our hands off each other. Sadly, we literally enforce a practice of abstinence, which communicates that humans are not trustworthy. Yet, as with so many other things, safety doesn't come from denying what we need. Trustworthy touch arises when we can work with different forms of contact without getting hurt. Moving toward strengthening our connections is a big step on the road to community health.

Father Prashant Olalaker, a Jesuit priest, claimed that a hand-to-hand dance was a turning point for him. It took place in a class where I invited people to join palms in a brief dance of blessing. I happened to be Father Prashant's partner. Reservations thwarted, he brought his hand to mine. A new world suddenly opened up to both of us. As a result of that hand-to-hand dance, Prashant later reflected, "Dance is a medium for peace.... When we restrict our communication to our intellect, disparities and conflict can arise from there, but when we interact at the level of the body, we interact as equals." This is the anecdotal experience of many people who enjoy a hand-to-hand dance for the first time.

What if a hand-to-hand dance could provide a revelatory way to explore and express your body's truth? What if you didn't have to learn ballroom dance, square dance, or salsa in order to connect with a partner? What if you didn't have to know fancy footwork to invite friends to dance in celebration? What if you could dance with a partner to pray for relationships? What if the Christian custom of "passing the peace" became a constant dance of peace? What if you could actually wrestle with God, community, a relationship, or a situation in a dance?

Any two hands can explore the power of human connection. The exercise below, which I sometimes refer to as "advanced handshaking," is a hand-to-hand dance of heart, eyes, and guts. When you connect with a partner, you can enter a profound yet manageable dance of intimacy.

Hand-to-Hand Dance

1. First, bring your palm to your partner's palm in a matter-of-fact way. No need to be mushy or sentimental. Notice the tactile sense in your hand. Is there warmth? Coolness? Other sensations?
2. Give your partner's hand a little push. (Encourage your partner not to be a pushover. It's okay to push back!)

3. Next, grab hold of your partner's wrist. Pull away from each other enough to feel your shared weight. You might get a wonderful stretch from this.

4. Return to a still, upright position, facing your partner. Join your palms again and let your two hands move together, following the connection. Let your hands take you off your spot on the floor, allowing your feet to follow.

5. Return to stillness again.

6. Starting with your palms together, make a different shape. Then make another shape. Surprise each other by quickly changing the shapes, faster than the speed of the mind.

7. Stop and hold still in one last shape.

8. Bring your hands back together, palm to palm.

9. Back away, opening the space between your hand and your partner's hand while keeping a feeling of overall connection.

10. When you are three or more feet apart, try this experiment. On the count of three, drop your hands and drop the feeling of being connected. Notice the difference. What is it like to release the feeling of being connected?

11. Restore the connection through space. On the count of three, release it again, allowing something bigger to hold the connection. Perhaps this is what faith feels like, trusting God to hold things.

12. Bring your palms back together one more time.

13. Put on some music and, for the length of the piece, let your hand-to-hand connection lead you in a spirited dance.

14. When the music is over, come to stillness.

15. Bow to your partner or give him a hug.

16. Take some time together to notice what it was like to follow the connection. Was it graceful or challenging? Were you able to breathe? Was there a moment where you felt particularly "at one"?

❖ ❖ ❖

One of the most magical parts of hand-to-hand dancing is how easily people become attuned to each other's force and speed. When we do this in my classes and workshops, people often exclaim, "I didn't know who was leading!" Experiencing physical harmony is like drinking an elixir of hope. Could it be that our bodies know how to find peace a thousand times faster than our analytical minds?

I find that when I reach across the river of life to connect with people who are different from me, I gain faith in our power to resolve conflicts, endure hardships, and walk new paths together. Whether I am wrestling with angels, healing a mistrust of intimacy, tending to my fear that no one will reach out and connect with me, or offering healing touch and creative friendship to those around me, a hand-to-hand dance with people I know—and with people I don't—directly connects me with a more generous universe. Love and joy once again seem possible. I may not remember the names of people I dance hand-to-hand with, but somehow our connections endure.

DANCING HEALTHY RELATIONSHIPS

When mother and baby are in close contact, the mother gazes at the child. The child connects, looking back. The child makes a sound; the mother follows, mimicking. The child is entranced. For a few seconds, child and mother blend their dance of gaze and coo with no thought about who is leading and who is following. They are entranced, attached. They become everything to each other. It's a holy communion.

Suddenly a door slams or the phone rings. The mother looks away. The baby's focus changes, too. When Mom looks back to her baby, the baby is no longer looking at her. Mom starts singing. The sound attracts the infant to look up and reach a tiny hand toward Mom's face. Mom follows the touch. With laughter, she pretends to eat the little hand. In this playful dance, they successfully reunite. Over and over throughout the day, if they are fortunate, they'll lead each other, follow, let go, move off in their own directions, and reunite.

This is the kind of dance that takes place for all of us, day after day, with other people, with pets, with groups, and with God. Neurologically, like the child and mother, we naturally practice the five movements of healthy relationships—leading, following, blending, letting go, and reuniting. When either partner gets insecure and overstresses any part of the dance, the relational dance breaks down. If we get stuck repeating one part of the dance to the exclusion of others, our physical, mental, and spiritual health pays the price. Our spirit depends on being able to spontaneously and successfully incorporate the whole range of these relational possibilities.

Practicing the five parts of this relationship dance at any time in our lives can help heal patterns in our behaviors and relationships that are out of balance, where one movement seems to dominate over the others. With practice, we can create the greater flow, harmony, fun, and cooperative spirit akin to communion, *shalom, salaam, Shanti, Paz,* even when there are upsets.

For a "healthy relationship checkup," practice all five movements: leading, following, blending, letting go, and reuniting.

LEADING

Leadership gets a lot of attention. Politicians, bosses, teachers, parents, and authorities of every kind "lead." It may surprise you to learn that all of us lead as well. Our voice, movement, words—even our stillness—are powerful factors in every dance of relationship. Some people influence everything around them by refusing to play. That leadership style is considered passive-aggressive.

Anything we originate is an initiation, a starting point, an idea. If we don't get hung up on feeling responsible for leading, we can enjoy an endless flow of ideas. Think for a moment about facial expressions. Children and actors have a vast repertoire of them. We, too, can cultivate endless ways of moving our facial muscles and get beyond judging any action as good or bad. It is much more fun to let ideas surface than to repress them. The more we entertain our ideas, the more energy we generate. And if someone else reinforces our ideas, our energy increases exponentially. Take laughter, for instance. Laughing is a great way to release and increase energy. Make weird faces, and you'll literally crack yourself up. Let someone else in on it, and the laughter will multiply. Test this out with another person or a small group of people and watch what happens.

Crazy Face Dance

~ Stand facing a partner and do a ten-second crazy "face dance." Faster than you can think, squirm your face in as many weird ways as you can.

~ Now move your facial muscles in slow ways. If this is hard, just move your mouth. Imagine all these movements as "ideas."

~ Watch your partner to see how long it takes for her to join you—or to laugh with you! It's almost impossible to do this without "leading" the other person into making facial movements, too.

Movement Blurts

~ Next, try some thirty-second movement "blurts." One partner moves in any way he wants to, and the other person just follows. Blurt it out! See what happens.

~ When you blurt, let go of worrying about your follower. Your only assignment is to *move*.

~ Switch roles.

~ If you don't feel like being that active, blurt in a quiet
way.

~ Afterwards, talk about what the experience was like
for each of you. What is it like to lead with a little
foolishness? Is it comfortable? Demanding?

❖ ❖ ❖

FOLLOWING

As much as each of us leads, we are also followers, devotees, fans,
groupies, and disciples. In fact, the word *disciple* means "to follow." "Follow the Leader" is one of the first games we learn, and
yet it is so much more. Those with the skills to consciously play
it can change their world.

In the Book of Ruth, Ruth followed Naomi. Defying cultural norms, she vowed, "Where you go, I will go ... your people
will be my people" (Ruth 1:16, NRSV). Similarly, Mary Magdalene
followed Jesus, washing and anointing his feet with expensive oil,
which garnered much criticism from the men around Jesus who
couldn't seem to match her bold, unequivocal response. Were
these women followers or leaders? Their actions tell us. These
women changed their world through physical acts of following.
It was not what they said that mattered most; it's what they did.

Following is proactive. It needn't be a duty. Dance takes this
further. It teaches us that moving with someone is a joy and a
privilege. When I give myself to another person's movements for
a time, I transcend myself and become part of something greater.
This kind of following is fun. For some of us, it's even ecstatic.
Rather than focusing on limits, ecstatic followers will cultivate a
Yes to whatever is there, physically responding with a sense of
abandon and joy. They jump in and support a person or a cause
with their whole being. Think of fans at a sports event, scream-

ing and jumping up and down as they follow the action. Their enthusiasm involves them fully and helps them "play along."

Joyfully reinforcing a particular movement or person also builds collective energy and influences ideas. This is what worship is about. "Going with" the Holy Other enhances what Jewish theologian Martin Buber called the I-Thou relationship. Following the principles and stories of a tradition with zeal invigorates love and fellowship.

When we are following, we are using our basic senses of seeing, hearing, tasting, touching, and smelling; our kinesthetic sense is activated as well. Tiny mirror neurons that read movement faster than the speed of the mind come into play. When someone suddenly falls, for example, we kinesthetically sense their movement in our muscles and breath. When a car suddenly swerves, we jump even though we may be a block away. Kinesthetic sensitivity is also how we empathize. If I am with someone in grief, I may feel a knot well up in my throat. Watching a person dance, I am more than audience; I share what she is going through.

As the old saying goes, "When one person suffers, everyone suffers. When one person rejoices, everyone rejoices." Any suffering that is kinesthetically communicated to us echoes in our body and boomerangs back to the other person. Suffering makes a complete round. The good news is that those who dance usually create the opposite of suffering; they create joy.

The old game of "Follow the Leader" is a great way to develop our understanding of this part of the dance of healthy relating. Notice that the game is not "Lead the Follower." Though we can emphasize both roles equally and learn where we feel greater comfort, following is a strength everyone needs. Perhaps your bodyspirit is an irrepressible inventor, as mine is. Or, perhaps you are more of a "go with the flow" person, happy to follow along. Building up both behaviors is necessary to dancing in partnership and vital to being able to follow a spiritual leader or principle.

Follow and Lead

1. With a companion, choose one person to lead and one person to follow.

2. For thirty seconds, whoever is the "leader" can move any way she likes, crazy or subtle. The other person's role is just to follow. It isn't important to follow exactly; following the *spirit* of the leader's movement is key. If the leader jumps and you have bad knees, it is perfectly fine to bounce instead of leap and still be "into" the movement.

3. Now reverse roles. Again, follow the spirit of the leader's actions. Notice if you prefer following or leading.

4. Try reversing roles once again, experimenting with leading and following in different ways: slow or fast, overt or subtle, moving side by side instead of looking across at each other, following from across a room.

5. Reflecting on this practice, relate it to your relationship with God, with leaders you follow, and even your home life. Is your followership a means of grace or a stumbling block for you?

❖ ❖ ❖

BLENDING

A third aspect in the dance of healthy partnering is blending. A zillion love songs laud the drive for the union that comes when two people's eyes meet and their bodies and spirits intertwine. One person may be shy or insecure and pull away, but that blending connection remains.

Blending is not only a result of mirroring; it goes beyond that. It's more like a chemical bond, a link, a friendly fusion, an attractive adherence of our atoms. It requires letting go of solo movement and "joining with." In the process, our navigational center shifts from inside our own solar plexus to a magnetic place between Me and You.

Sacred, covenantal relationships, like marriage or religious commitment, arise from our deepest and most lasting unions. Some people may taste blessed union only once or twice, not knowing how physically accessible and basic the palpable phenomenon of blending is. Yet synchronizing is as natural as breathing. The intensity of our gratitude for this physical experience may vary, but it is available all the time. It's in the way we are designed; blending starts in our bodies. You can discover this all on your own.

Dancing in Sync

~ Bring one hand in the air. Let it move smoothly.

~ Bring your other hand alongside it, moving in coordination with the first.

~ Enjoy moving your arms in parallel fashion.

~ Release any notion of one hand following the other. Even as two different hands, they'll continue to dance symbiotically.

❖ ❖ ❖

Like singers blending in harmony, physical rapport with another person feeds our longing for union and cocreation. Physical rapport tells us that we are not alone. Gina Mausner, founder of Pilot Your Power Now, identifies three keys for creating rapport: *sensory acuity*—using our senses to notice other people's behavior; *matching and mirroring*—matching or following someone's mood, posture, face, voice, breath, and actions; and *pacing and leading*—matching someone's intensity level and leading him to another state. These keys can be easily translated to a movement level.

When I "sync up" with my InterPlay colleague, Phil, in a dance, we share an incredible connection. Occasionally, it feels as though, instead of wandering the earth with one wing, we each find our other wing and rise on two wings of joy. A woman who saw us dance told us how deeply moved she was by the visceral, playful connection she witnessed. I can feel it. When Phil and I dance together, it is a kind of elevator ride to higher consciousness. It is remarkable to know that it is apparent to others.

The beauty of the blending dance is that neither partner need get stuck in a leader or follower role. The joy is in the freedom to do both. The level of enjoyment and connection varies, but the possibility of creating rapport with *anyone* becomes evident. Buber's classic *I and Thou* speaks of the person-divine interaction as if it were the utterance of a single, holy word or as a unified synchronous act of being. He writes, "The primary word I-Thou can be spoken only with the whole being. Concentration and fusion into the whole being can never take place through my agency, nor can it ever take place without me. I become through my relation to the Thou; as I become I, I say Thou. All real living is meeting."

We can't force this experience, but it is very easy to invite it on a physical level. Playing with the keys of rapport, we can sense our partner's mood, mirror and match her actions, and meet her intensity. In the process we can encounter the dyadic consciousness of blending that is so crucial to feeling at one with others, the world, and God.

Dancing in Rapport

~ Choose a piece of music that is harmonious.

~ With a companion, come palm to palm.

~ Let your hands move together.

~ Instead of thinking about who is leading or following, simply focus on following either partner's actions as they present themselves.

~ Don't worry about giving equal time or trading off roles. And, please don't cue each other with words. Your body is wise. Let it prove this to you.

~ Your hands may come apart as you continue following and leading.

~ If you find the magical blended feeling where you are uncertain who is leading, enjoy!

~ As you end, bow or thank your partner.

~ Take a few moments to notice any highlights from the dance. Have you had similar experiences before? What would it be like to follow, lead, and blend with God in this manner as a way to pray, or to bless someone you love?

❖ ❖ ❖

It is possible to extend leading, following, and blending to a group. Wing It! Performance Ensemble practices these skills to perform dances that have no preset choreography. The choreography happens in the moment as dancers initiate, follow, and cocreate solos, duets, and trios. Ten or more members of the ensemble "tune in" to the bigger picture of actions and meanings. As a company member, I've learned that my cohorts are more than trustworthy. They are the art and the artist at once. Developing the capacity of groups to embody this kind of fullness in our everyday lives has become a passion for me. When we do it, we find levels of success and community that promote our highest collective good.

LETTING GO

In our hunger for peace, we may think of unity as the ultimate destiny. The only problem is that, once we are there, we start to fidget. No one likes getting stuck in a place where everyone must conform and commit to certain emotions and behaviors. Humans are not lemmings. We resist cultishness just as we resent loss of communion.

At some point in the dance of relationship, someone will change the action and break away from blending. Breaking away is part of freedom. In psychological terms, this is the ability to differentiate. We are not supposed to be identical to anyone else. We are each unique creatures, in spite of tenacious tendencies to hang onto another human, a place, a pet, or God.

Being able to let go in the dance of partnership is just as important as being able to follow and blend. Glomming on and clutching restrict the flow of grace. Overattaching enforces nothing but a breathless security where our bodies trade healthy relating for that human invention, psychic incarceration.

For many of us, it's hard to let go. Perhaps this is why there are so many spiritual teachings about it. The famous mystic St. John of the Cross said, "Love consists not in feeling great things but in having great detachment ... for until the cord be broken, the bird cannot fly."

The slogan "Let go and let God" reminds us that we always have to move on in dances, relationships, and life. It happens when kids grow up, when a partner leaves, when a job ends, when we move across town, even when we turn and face a new direction during the course of the day. Change is inevitable. As a person who has been married for thirty years to one man, and working for thirty years with another, commitment is the one constant I have had. But I have learned to let go of ideas, control, directions—sometimes even the future of these relationships—in order to let them "dance." Counselors John Landgraf and Carroll Wright offer, "That which you hold, you lose. That which you resist, remains. That to which you are attached, imprisons. That which you surrender frees. Embrace whatever comes. Flow with whatever happens. Understand whatever arises. Learn from each crisis you meet."

I believe this gets easier when we know how to physically improvise with change, when to follow, when to lead, and when to let go. Letting go is not falling into an abyss. Try this physical action: Close your hand. Open it. Close it. Open it. Both actions are possible all the time. An open hand makes it easier to grasp each new moment. Letting go of positions and connections that we are holding allows us to dance the next new step and develop the faith muscles to trust that the dance of life will continue, no matter what happens.

One of the easiest ways to detach and let go is to have a little fun, to get tricky. Trickster energy plays with us and forces change. Life and Spirit like to throw us curves and crazy moves. Tricking a partner in a follow-and-lead dance helps both partners detach, shift, and respect the individuality of the other. In moments of letting go, partners perk up. Energy and fun loosen us up. Trickiness can be our treat.

Trick to Treat

1. With a partner, join your palms.
2. Follow the connection and blend your movements.
3. Next, try to trick your partner. You hardly have to think about it. Everyone is an expert trickster. Here are a few examples:
   ~ For ten seconds, poke, tickle, run away.
   ~ Change quickly or break away.
   ~ Stop dancing altogether and let your partner dance alone for a moment.
4. What happens when you trick each other? Does it feel wild? Too wild? Fun? Liberating? Rebellious? Normal? What role does poking fun have in your relationships? How do you feel when you get poked or played with?

❖ ❖ ❖

Have you ever experienced the Holy as a Trickster? I think the Divine is like a wise guru who knows how and when to "trick" followers into selfhood. In my dance with God, the Holy repeatedly puts power in my hands right when I am working on not being so controlling. Once, in a guided meditation, my Higher Power asked me to hold a sword. I wanted to hand it back. "I am not trustworthy," I thought. But God insisted. Apparently, I had to be shown that I needed to have my power in hand in order not to use it on someone. "Don't be powerful" was not an option.

Letting go doesn't have to be aggressive. In movement terms, it can be as simple as releasing the connection and dancing on your own for a moment. We can learn to do this with playful practice and skillful consciousness. Anne Morrow Lindbergh's *Gift from the Sea*, read at many a wedding, shows her understanding of this healthy aspect of dancing in partnership:

> A good relationship has a pattern like a dance and is built on some of the same rules. The partners do not need to hold on tightly, because they move confidently in the same pattern, intricate but gay and swift and free, like a country-dance of Mozart's. To touch heavily would be to arrest the pattern and freeze the movement, to check the endlessly changing beauty of its unfolding. There is no place here for the possessive clutch, the clinging arm, the heavy hand; only the barest touch in passing. Now arm in arm, now face-to-face, now back-to-back—it does not matter which. Because they know they are partners moving to the same rhythm, creating a pattern together, and being invisibly nourished by it.

REUNITING

Sometimes we get stuck in the tricking mode or in a state of rebellion. *Rebellion* means "war against," and it's a hard place to live. How do we make our way back if we've made a serious break from others or lost our connection through distractions? In times of anger or confusion, we often isolate ourselves and get stuck outside the dance.

After struggling and spending money for counseling, I was at a breaking point, ready to give up on one of my dearest relationships. Instead, my friend suggested that we dance hand to hand.

Although hesitant, I'm glad I chose to practice what I preach. With music playing, my friend lifted a palm. I brought mine into contact with his. Tears rolled down my face as tenderness was offered. As our hands traced our connection, I remembered many journeys we'd taken. Our bodies knew the dances of invention and grounding. As we moved, connection was restored. Where attempts at words failed us, the dance of leading, following, blending, letting go, and reuniting soothed my anxious heart. Afterwards, we were able to start over and rededicate ourselves to the work at hand. All because my friend offered a simple physical practice, an entry into reunion, and I walked through that entryway.

If you get tricked, left behind, or experience changes in the dance, reuniting can be as simple—and as challenging—as reaching out and offering a hand. This may be easy if you are not too attached to a partner, but when you have a lot to lose, you may have to shoosh the voices of hurt, temper your mixed feelings, or humble yourself.

For those in conflict, reunion is more likely to occur with a handshake, as many schoolteachers know. When we reach out to touch another, we reinvigorate relationship. The movement of reuniting can be shockingly graceful and effortless. Dancing, once again, helps us practice and believe in the sacred dance of partnering.

Dancing Reunion

1. Bring your palm to your partner's palm.
2. Open the space between your palms while still maintaining a sense that your palms are connected.
3. Together count to three and drop the connection at the same time.
4. After a few moments, one partner raises his hand in connection through space.
5. Then, the second partner's hand rises and connects across the space.

6. Practice dropping and reconnecting a few times.

7. Turn away from and back to your partner as you play with dropping and reconnecting.

8. Put on some music. In a hand-to-hand or follow-the-leader dance with your partner, include the full menu of movement possibilities: leading, following, blending, letting go, and reuniting.

9. As you move, both of you will contribute to matching and shifting to new ideas. There may even be brief solos in which one or both of you move on your own.

10. When the music ends, notice and reflect on the experience of dancing with this person on this occasion. Was it easy and coordinated? Were there awkward moments? Were there highlights? Did you sense the spectrum of possibilities needed for healthy relationships with people, even with God?

❖ ❖ ❖

Most spiritual traditions suggest that God is always there. Unlike our human counterparts and even our unpredictable earth, God's partnering is steadfast. Though we may drop the connection and claim to dance on our own, the Universal Source of unconditional love inspires the freedom to dance solo, rebel, and reconcile over and over. When we dance these practices of healthy relationship, I believe it pleases God enormously.

Lead, follow, blend, let go, reunite—these five movements help us live, practice, and dance in all relationships. If we can dance each part, we are capable of integrating them into a whole. The sacred dance of beloved community awaits us when we do.

DANCING IN COMPANY

White umbrella, white banners, white dresses, white shirts, dark skin glistening, one body moving slowly out of the dark into the light. Stepping on the same beat, on the same foot, amazing grace swings the procession, and the shadowy wing of the theater releases them to us. As they have a thousand times before, they enter as our ancestors, a cloud of witnesses, dancing saints. Their beauty is unmistakable. Somehow everyone knows we belong with them.

We are seeing *Revelations*. Alvin Ailey created his masterpiece during the civil rights movement, and this suite of dances proclaims the transcendence of a people beaten down but bent on glory. Accompanied by traditional gospel songs, like "I Been 'Buked," "Wade in the Water," "Fix Me Jesus," and "You May Run On," the dances are a liturgy of soul. With every piece, the audience anticipates the "Rocka My Soul" finale—thirty exuberant dancers in their "All shall be revealed" glory. When the time comes, audiences around the globe jump to their feet in a standing ovation, clapping to the music, joining in the dance. We are part of what Alvin Ailey dancers refer to as "The Company," the company of God's beloved ones.

Humans are inseparable from community, just as planets are from galaxies. Ejecting ourselves is impossible. The sorrow of being exiled, shunned, imprisoned, or divorced tells us so. Were we mere individuals, we could leave groups without suffering. Instead, we know our connection acutely, recognizing how much we need the company we keep.

Constantly looking to "belong," and wanting ways to energize and strengthen community, we sometimes catch brief glimpses of a higher communal plane: A rock star "raises the roof" and gets us dancing in the aisles; we are part of a wave at a stadium; we watch Olympic-sized spectacles of Taiko drummers and beautifully costumed dancers running to the center of an arena en masse. There is such power in numbers!

Are we part of this company? Yes! The skills of dancing with one other person extend to dancing with the many. All the practices we do alone are enhanced in company.

Dance is communal. Like naming yourself, marrying yourself, performing your own heart surgery, or birthing a child, some things obviously need others. Perhaps that's why dance is having a comeback. Twenty-first-century citizens who hum along on technological networks are facing globe-sized problems that cell phones and the Internet can't solve. We need each other in real, close-to-the-ground ways. And when we dance together, we turn the world around. A spiritual revolution is a movement in the making.

Dancing not only unifies community, it behaves like one of those old telephone company switchboards and patches you into a "party line" or a "conference call" of the spirit. Most Western-educated people have retired the old dance switchboard as "useless," but some still know its secret. Dancing empowers cellular communication of the body. Its ancient telecommunication technology works.

I no longer dismiss the power of kinesthetic communication. In a yearlong group, a different dancer each month had a loved one who was close to death. Each time we danced on behalf of one of them, time and again, the dancer's relative let go, died, or made a significant shift within hours of the group's efforts. We began to joke about our power to dance people to the other side.

Dancing taught me that I could tune in to the energetic presence of friends even when they were far away. I can sense if they are "off the grid," and later confirm that they were on retreat, absorbed in a project, taking "downtime," or ill.

Dancing one morning, I asked companions to dance on behalf of my mother and other people with Alzheimer's disease. As I watched them form healthy bonds of movement and breath, it made me think of healthy brains. I closed my eyes and proposed this health to my mother's brain. That evening when I called her partner, he exclaimed that she'd had an unusually "normal" day. What a welcome reprieve!

As we practice the skills of listening to our body wisdom, moving, breathing, and being present, miracles seem eminently possible. As it is said, "Where two or three are gathered in my name, there am I in the midst of you" (Matthew 18:20, NRSV).

Two practices can help us tune into the wider community: easy focus and "attuning." When we get overly focused on visualizing and analyzing, we tend to downplay our connection with other senses. Playing with easy focus gets us out of our separate boxes and opens us to the wider web. It only takes a little practice to open up to the big dance.

Easy Focus Dance

~ Take a deep breath, sigh, and shake out your limbs and voice.

~ Bring your hands to your "focuser" (that scrunchy place between your eyes where worries tend to collect) and give it a "wheeeee."

~ Expand your gaze to include your peripheral awareness.

~ Notice your hearing, smelling, and kinesthetic sensing. Check in and "listen" to your body.

~ Think of a person. As you consider this person, do you sense a connection? Is it weak, strong, or nonexistent?

~ To strengthen the connection, dance on her behalf, sending her gratitude and love.

❖ ❖ ❖

Using your following and blending skills, you can become attuned to others in creative ways. Forming an instant dance company, like a pickup choir, is a fun way to pray and support the different concerns and needs of group members. Consider how geese fly in formation: "Going with" a leader makes it possible to choreograph in the moment and gain strength in numbers.

Gesture Choir

~ Gather with a group of at least two others.

~ Put on some music and, with one mover in front and the others behind, form a flock for a "gesture choir."

~ As the front mover moves, the followers "attune" to the dancer. As much as possible, incorporate the movements of the leader as if they were your own. Move in harmony with the leader. With easy focus, release the need to look at the leader directly; simply follow the idea of the movement. Slow or rhythmic movement patterns are easiest to match, but followers can adapt the movements as needed.

~ When the music ends, rest and notice.

~ Invite another person to "lead the choir," dancing for joy, celebration, lament, rage, or in prayer.

~ Rest and take notice again. What did you become aware of as you tuned in to the leader? Did you feel in company with the other dancers? Was it easy or hard for you to feel "in sync"?

❖ ❖ ❖

DANCING THE FUTURE

The current task of humanity is to tend the body of the earth— its creatures, flora, and humanity. As populations increase, and land, food, and water grow scarce, not only can we not afford any more corporate soul loss or recklessness in our relationships, we need to make an evolutionary leap for the good of humanity. Love is that leap. As the poet W. H. Auden wrote, "We must love each other or die."

Daniel Goleman and fellow researchers of social intelligence think we are preparing for this leap as we knit together our neurological "low roads and high roads." "Low roads" literally arise in the lower back of the brain, transporting emotion, automatic responses, and body-to-body communication. Their communications work fast and come easy. "High road" functioning uses the front of the brain to help access conscious choices that require deliberation, inhibition, and analysis. Goleman posits that the "social brain" of the future will bring these two systems into a single dimension through "fluid and wide-ranging neural networks that synchronize around relating to others."

As a modern dancer, I believe that this is exactly what happens in conscious dancing: We synchronize when we relate to others. Imagine a gospel choir. Setting up a common pulse, they shift weight from one leg back to the other. Movement and beat attune bodies and souls to one another. As the choir sings, the meaning of the words transports them, in unison, to a higher level of intention. As members send their message outward, emotions and body communication synchronize with conscious choices to serve a unifying purpose.

Swiss psychologist Carl Jung coined the term *collective unconscious* to describe an enormous physical reservoir of hidden meanings that influence and shape group awareness in a culture. I believe that dancing tends to coordinate and propel this unconscious dimension into visibility. When people have lost touch with their kinesthetic and emotional intelligence, reintroducing dance as a spiritual practice often helps them recover their unquenchable thirst for body-to-body affiliation.

I see it over and over again in a simple group activity that we do in InterPlay, called "Walk, Stop, and Run." It's an improvisational form that affirms individual fullness and choice, as it coordinates high levels of fluidity and synchronicity. I think of it as a folk dance for this new era. The directions are simple and pedestrian, but the results in a group can be amazing. Here are the instructions:

Walk, Stop, and Run

~ Walk in any direction.
~ Change directions.
~ Walk in unusual paths.

~ Find the edges of the space as well as the middle.

~ Walk backward. If you run into someone, say "Thank you."

~ Stop. Simply stand, rest, and be near others.

~ Walk forward again in any direction.

~ Walk right by others, barely missing them.

~ If you can, run. (People are brilliant at avoiding collision.)

~ Walk at your own pace.

~ Follow someone.

~ Put on music and play for a moment with walking, stopping, running—and with each other.

~ When the music ends, take some time to notice your experience. What was it like to be in the group? Were there moments of community? Could you follow, lead, blend, and go on your own way? What was it like to have this much freedom? Was it too much or do you find yourself craving more?

❖ ❖ ❖

Walking, stopping, and running lead to all manner of movement and connections with people we wouldn't ordinarily hang out with. Everyone feels included. Afterwards, people notice more energy and connection. The greater the willingness to play, the more miraculous the results. As they acclimate to this process, they go beyond thinking about how they are moving and enter into synchronous group rituals.

Witnesses remark, "It seemed so choreographed," yet group coordination is never forced. When individuals act for themselves in collective creativity, they naturally integrate as "wholes in the whole." This is why Walk, Stop, and Run often becomes a favorite ritual form for gathering, bonding, praying, grieving, and sharing concerns. It isn't the walking, stopping, or running that makes it so powerful; it's the synchronous flow of people coming together, moving apart, and connecting their intentions together in corresponding shapes and dynamics.

We used this form when a friend was tragically killed in an accident. Fifteen of us gathered to memorialize her. An altar was set up in the middle of the room, and along one wall were some of her belongings, photos, and words. We spent time viewing and holding scarves, hair clips, flyers, poems, prayer icons, and other things she'd left behind. Then we began our ritual. We took deep breaths together and warmed up, stretching and moving until we were fully engaged. As we walked, stopped, and moved around the room, we brought her belongings to the altar, each person sharing one memory in three sentences. Over the next ten minutes, a collective body memory of this woman assembled. Some people moved continuously. Several sat peacefully. Everyone paused whenever someone spoke. Dancing memorialized our deceased friend in act and word.

What if communities could dance in strength, love, joy, and grace? What if we could embrace the tricksters in our midst as instigators who teach us to let go, open up, and begin afresh? What if we could follow, lead, and dance in physical contact to bless, heal, and remember who we are? What if dancing were God making love to us?

A dozen hands might come together, each person bringing one hand to the middle of a circle, in contact with the other hands. In a circle of friendship, music playing, our hands would flow in connection, then fly like birds and swim around each other like fish, darting and diving. There would be moments of stillness and frenzy, craziness and quietude. Some hands would take off and leave the circle, then return. Mesmerized by our dancing hands, we might for a moment let ourselves play freely. If we were to dance this dance again, after hearing stories, witnessing sacred movements, and listening with our heart, we might begin to see this dance as proof of a beloved company.

CHAPTER EIGHT

DANCING AS PEACEMAKING

All the people were dancing
leaves, olive branches in their hands.
Precise steps, histories, creeds
None of it mattered anymore.
                    —*Cynthia Winton-Henry*

The great theologian Teilhard de Chardin once said, "Someday after mastering the winds, the waves, the tides and gravity, we shall harness for God the energies of Love, and then for the second time in the history of the world we will have discovered fire."

I believe that those who discover dancing as a spiritual practice harness energies of love. We ignite the fire of peace that is needed to navigate ordinary, everyday conflict, as well as avoid large-scale violence. I am talking about dancing that moves in relation to the earth, to each other, and God, from moment to moment, embodying real acts of faith.

In the late seventies and early eighties, six women were murdered on Mt. Tamalpais in Marin County, California. The local community was devastated. Dancer Anna Halprin and her husband, Lawrence, were leading a workshop at the time, and the workshop participants wanted to do something to reclaim the mountain from the horror of the killing. They created a ritual dance that involved walking along the trails where the killings had occurred. Ironically, a few days after the performance of this ritual dance, the killer was caught. Peace returned to the mountain.

When Anna told this story to Don Jose Mitsuwa, a Huichol shaman who was 109 years old at the time, he said, "This mountain is one of the most sacred places on earth. I believe in what your people did, but to be successful in purifying this mountain, you must return to it and dance for five years." And so the "Circle the Earth" dance was born. Every spring, the dance ritual continues and expands. Halprin says that it calls upon a Higher Power in "a series of moving ceremonies and prayers. Most importantly, it is witnessed by people who understand and support its purpose." What had once been a dance to reclaim a small measure of peace on one community's mountain has become a dance to restore peace to the planet.

When we coordinate our movement, we balance our hostilities, reignite our enthusiasm to be together, and kinesthetically awaken our empathy and openness. Whether we're dancing hand to hand with another person or in a room of fellow movers, practicing the five movements of healthy relationship in community—leading, following, blending, letting go, and reuniting—dancing demands cooperation and constant reconciliation. When we dance, we have to leap barriers with folks we may not be attracted to, agree with, or even know. Yet our physical commitment to push, pull, link, and be drawn into common movements can nurture and keep the peace.

Sometimes, dancing for peace is overt. More often, peace is a subtext of dancing. Dancing *keeps* the peace. I saw this vividly demonstrated in the spiral dance of indigenous people in India. In their ancient religious dance, standing sideways hip to hip—alternating a young man, then a woman, then a man, and so on—they interlock arms so tightly around each other's waists that one misstep throws off the whole line. Running sideways full tilt to mesmerizing music, on cue, they suddenly switch directions. They must harmonize. The dancing back and forth, the exertion, the stamina, and the beauty of this dance are replicated in their painting and philosophy of life. In a community hall in Tillasari, Western India, the spiral dance is painted on every wall. The Jesuit priests who helped build the hall honor this symbol as a different expression of communion and have painted it in their own chapels.

Pleasing forms of aesthetic, physical coordination in groups are becoming an imperative as populations increase and resources decrease. People who live in countries like India and Thailand already know how to harmonize movement effortlessly on jammed streets. Driving on their roads is like a wild walking-stopping-running dance. A Westerner's response would be fear of collision and road rage, but these people know that if they had to protect their own space at every turn, they'd be exhausted. Instead, every moving vehicle seems to dance. I'll never forget the night I hopped aboard a rickshaw in Mumbai with two friends. The driver had the wheel, and I had to abandon control. He danced us hilariously through the streets, turned up the music, laughed, and called out to other drivers. Buzzing through smog, frenzy, insanity, as our driver bobbled his crazy head, swerving, stopping at a light just in time, our rickshaw became a free radical of joy in the hands of a conscious lunatic calling out for the entire world to play. How like life with God! This was peace beyond my wildest imagining. We were dancing.

As I travel and see the way that dance moves people beyond divisions, I have all the evidence I need to know that we can reclaim the power of movement as a peacemaking spiritual practice that is not only good for *our* soul, it is good for *all* souls. I often think to myself, "If only I could show people what I've learned." In my extremely diverse city of Oakland, many awake, socially conscious, disenfranchised people segregate and lick their wounds. How miraculous, then, when white, black, and brown, Christian, Jewish, Wiccan, and Interfaith people drop into dance studios to move together in freedom and joy. The peacemaking dancers commit to something more than tolerance. Creating and living in peace—this dream is possible.

Conflict, say the experts, is natural. Quantum physicists like David Bohm, Fritjof Capra, and Gary Zukav describe the reality of the universe as one interconnected dance: At some level our bodies, thoughts, and world are made up of this dance of energy, continually annihilating and creating. As such, it is unrealistic to think that we can end conflict. Given the instincts of territoriality, human psychology, and the fact of accidents, we can't help but interfere in each other's patterns. Learning to dance with these conflicts should be our goal.

All over the world, indigenous and modern people incorporate dancing for peacekeeping and peacemaking. UNESCO, the United Nations, and the National Endowment for the Arts fund programs in which dance artists teach conflict resolution and mediation. Universities, institutes, and enlightened religious groups also include dancing as a language and strategy for peace. Although the West has only acknowledged dance as a subject worth studying for the last fifty years or so, Sangita Shresthova aptly reminds us, in her article "What is Endangered Dance?" that over the eons, in Eastern traditions, dance is regarded as the "apotheosis of human knowledge." Sacred dance, in particular, passes on humanity's most principled values.

Martin Luther King, Jr. and Mahatma Gandhi, icons of peacemaking, may not have been called dancers, but they knew that power lies in what we embody. Rooted in spiritual ideals of respect for differences and dreams of joyful cooperation, they preached and taught that peace is reflected in how we move in the world. Acting accordingly, they disciplined their personal movements and inspired collective practices that became unstoppable. As seen among the South Africans who danced through the streets to oppose apartheid, bodies and souls that demonstrate in peace eventually create peace. Dancing is a powerful way to invoke a peaceful order.

But with generations of pain and assault between people and groups, trying to answer God's invitation—"Will you dance?"—can be hard. Our bodies are tight with anger and fear. "Will you dance with your enemy?" is like being told to love your enemy, a radical religious suggestion for building a peaceable kingdom. To move in this direction, each of us needs to remember that our body is not a battleground, as writer and activist Gayle Brandeis posits in her award-winning poem, "A Body Politic of Peace." She beautifully conveys the vision of peace as "the body's natural state" and rings the bell of the hope that infuses dance for peacemaking:

> Listen.
> The body is not
> a battleground,
> as some people
> would like you
> to believe.
> The body knows
> peace; peace, after
> all, is the body's
> natural state.
> Think of the body
> in repose, the way
> muscles loosen,
> breath opens up;
> think of the body
> in love. It knows
> what to do. It is
> our mind that does
> not. It is our mind
> that makes us feel
> separate, isolated,
> it is our mind
> that dreams up war.

The body says no,
come back to me,
I am fragile and strong
and I connect you
to your brothers and sisters.
I connect you to the earth.
Come back to the heartbeat,
the pulse, the rhythm
we all walk to, regardless
of nation or color. Come back
to the breath—inhale, take the world
deep into your lungs; exhale,
give yourself back fully.
This is what the body says:
release the peace
that lives within your skin.

CULTIVATING PERSONAL PEACE ONE DANCE AT A TIME

At one time in my life, dancing was the only place I sensed the possibility of peace. It healed my wounds and helped release the obstacles my body had inherited from generational wounds. At each step in my development, my dedication to freedom and peace in the world intensified. Dancing became my form of activism. Because of my addictive tendencies to overdo everything, I put twelve-step practices alongside dancing and InterPlay, and I was constantly reminded to let go and let God. That is when the dream of peace became most real for me. That of which I had dared not dream became a reality.

My hope for you is that the dance practices in this book can cultivate peace for you in the following ways.

Use dance to cultivate personal peace. "Let peace begin on earth, let it begin with me," say the lyrics of a popular song. Employing everything from the meditative one-hand dance to an exformational dance that can clear you of challenging emotions, movement can help recenter you in your body and unlock your innate wisdom. This peace is the peace to be who you are without worry. It is not a staged or pious peace. It isn't forced or controlled. It is a personal peace that, as Gayle's poem puts it, loosens you and brings you back to the heartbeat of humanity. To develop peace in yourself makes you the best peace mediator you can be. As Kenneth Cloke, director of the Center for Dispute Resolution, says, "It is easier to assist conflicted parties in being authentic and centered with one another if we are authentic and centered [ourselves]."

Use dance to meet your basic psychological needs. As dancing increases physical ease between people, it addresses what psychiatrist William Glasser calls the four basic psychological needs that guide all behaviors: "Belonging—fulfilled by loving, sharing and cooperating. Inner Power—fulfilled by achieving, accomplishing, being recognized and respected. Freedom—fulfilled by making choices. Fun—fulfilled by laughing and playing."

I wholeheartedly concur! Remember the three master keys from chapter 3, "Unlocking the Dance of Joy"? The grace key (the physicality of grace), the maker key (the power of kinesthetic imagination), and the fun-lover key (the joy of play) all unlock the doors of body and soul. Add in the five recommended daily requirements for health that I mentioned in chapter 5, "Dancing for Healing"—moving, vocalizing, telling your story, receiving contact, and just being with others—and they all add up to ways you can meet your core psychological needs in tangible, life-changing ways.

Use dance to release negative emotional buildup. As the Dalai Lama suggests, "To make peace in the Middle East, we must decrease negative emotions." This is good advice not only on a national but also a personal level. I think of my husband. When he is distressed about work, he gets depressed. But when he does an exformational dance, letting his frustration come out in crazy sounds and faces, letting his whole body dance, his experience shifts. Immediately afterwards, he sighs and says, "That feels better." The negative emotions have moved on.

When African bushmen experience a conflict, their elders convene a *xotla*, a public meeting that all adults attend. The parties are allowed to express grievances before the assembled community. Sometimes their group tensions are best resolved through dance. As people sing and clap, while the dancers dance, the *xotla* can go on for days, until all parties literally exhaust their negative feelings.

One women's spirituality group uses another strategy for tension. Mad? "Sing it! You won't be able to stay mad." I would add, "Move it!" If you can let your body speak, once it's had its say, most often you'll want to move on.

Use dance to increase your problem-solving skills. Those accustomed to using creativity and imagination recognize that there are multiple answers to a problem. Dancing can switch you into a higher-functioning mode and lead to new ideas and behaviors. Literally pulling you out of your "box," movements take on a "trickster" role, leading to understandings you didn't expect. Using any process that requires you to let go of your agenda, play with resistances, or merely distract you can lead you to new solutions, theories, and relationships.

A 2009 study, cited in *Science Daily*, showed that simply by swinging their arms participants were better able to solve a complex problem. Psychology professor Alejandro Lleras observed, "People tend to think that their mind lives in their brain, dealing in conceptual abstractions, very much disconnected from the body. This emerging research is fascinating because it is demonstrating how your body is a part of your mind in a powerful way.

The way you think is affected by your body and, in fact, we can use our bodies to help us think."

On another note, some decisions are so arbitrary that it's ridiculous to let them exacerbate tension. The Rock-Paper-Scissors (RPS) game is described as a "dance of hands" that has long been used to settle disputes where mediation would not suffice. The world's leading RPS authority, a Canadian named Graham Walker, calls it "the most elegant and profound of all conflict-resolution processes." It just shows that when you turn something into a nonverbal gesture, it suddenly gets easier.

Use dance to subvert and avoid words of judgment. In a handout called "Curtains!" Russell Brunson, Zephryn Conte, and Shelley Masar list judgment calls that "close the curtain" on conversation. Maybe you'll recognize some of these all-too-familiar words: "You must ... You have to ... If you don't, then ... Don't ask questions ... Don't you realize ... You're just trying to." Reading the list reminds me of the minefields in our speech. As you may know all too well, the verbal challenge in peacemaking can be the most difficult; talk can get you into trouble.

Movement is sneaky. Because it can level the communication playing field, especially when you don't rely on performing prescribed steps, dancing can move you toward your emotional intelligence, which makes it easier to feel and share at a deeper level. Uttering no words at all is sometimes an advantage.

Use dance to redirect disdainful actions. In *Dancing in Conflict,* Patrick Koop, founder of the Peace Agents Foundation, reflects on aikido, a Japanese martial art created as an art of peace by Moriher Yesheiba during World War II in one of the darkest periods of human history. Koop says aikido teaches people "not to look at the opponent as an enemy," but to focus on "neutralizing destructive energies." He describes the movement as a "step in or step out" to "outbalance the opponent." Fifth-degree black belt holder George Leonard puts it this way: "The genius of aikido is to transform the most violent attack, by embracing it, into a dance."

Similarly, when you dance, you can pay attention to energy, step in or away when a conflict exceeds your capacity, and learn to move *with* rather than *against* the people around you.

Use dance to create distance from conflict zones. To step away from geographies of pain is a basic principle of reducing conflict. Something as simple as stepping back or walking away from aggression is a reliable strategy. Taking this one step further, when you make a neutral place, a dance zone, you can soften up tensions. This is one purpose of a ritual environment. It can allow you and the one you're in conflict with to reflect, choose how to act according to a higher good, rehearse and even transform your way of acting.

Rituals both set apart and bind together our experiences. Trying to create peace in a place where hatred runs rampant is like putting medicine in a bleeding wound. Not until the wound is bound up and has had time to close can you treat it. A dance can be an act of binding or a means of taking pressure off a wound. It is necessary to let peace and love dance the other areas of the body, lest the whole body become a war zone.

Use dance to help you forgive and move forward. One of the most difficult steps in peacemaking is to show up after you've been hurt. I was furious when the head of a dance organization banned my friend over a piece of choreography. As soon as I heard about it, I spoke my mind. Disgusted with the organization's judgmental response, I indignantly withdrew my membership. Years later, the dance group coaxed me to return. The invitation was compelling, and I wanted to forgive and forget. I agreed to give it a try. On the first night, the dancing began and I wept. I remembered that these dancers were like my extended spiritual family. I had left over a shortcoming. In dancing, my animosity finally melted, I confessed my sorrow aloud, and the rift was healed. Dancing led the way.

Rose Berger and Julie Polter visited Corrymeela, Cornerstone Community, and Currach in Northern Ireland where Catholics and Protestants touch "fingertips in an arch over the desolate cyclone fencing, razor wire, and bricks of the 'peace line.'" They saw dances of peace being enacted where "memory-carrying people can remember yet forgive, where human frailty and weighted histories might turn in a fresh step, where the bones of Northern Ireland, dry for so long in broken tenements and divided suburbs, may yet raise themselves up ... as they strive to translate small reconciling gestures into oratorios of movement." This was more than poetry for them. These people literally danced forgiveness.

Inner Peace Dance: 80 Percent Stillness

~ Take a deep breath. Let it out with a sigh.

~ With one arm or your whole body, make a shape.

~ Breathe into the shape, becoming present to it.

~ Shifting from one shape or posture to another, it is important to indulge the stillness.

~ Incorporating music, dance with 80 percent stillness (or whatever is the best percentage for you right now). Your shapes can transition with quick energetic shifts or slow ones.

~ It is essential to breathe. Sometimes sighing or toning while moving keeps the breath alive and the quiet energy flowing.

~ Dancing with gestures and stillness, invite forgiveness for yourself or others. Lift those you cannot forgive to your higher power.

~ If you like, imagine creating ripples of peace out into the world.

❖ ❖ ❖

DANCING PEACE ON A LARGER SCALE

On a more collective level, Samuel Lewis, founder of the Dances of Universal Peace, traveled the globe in the 1960s and 1970s, studying the esoteric sects of the world's orthodox religions and teaching Sufism to young Americans radicalized by the draft and the Vietnam War. Lewis saw the need to redirect negative energy and eventually married mysticism to movement to "promote peace through the arts." In a newspaper article, Gail Sickel shared her observation of "The Dances": "The dances bring forth an experience that's heartfelt. I notice the faces of people who come. When they arrive, they're tense. When they leave, they're so relaxed, because the idea is to internalize joy, to feel one's self." The Dances of Universal Peace draw on hundreds of simple dances and chants from every religious tradition, focusing on both inner and outer peace. The chants include sacred phrases in a wide range of languages, including Arabic, Aramaic, English, Hawaiian, Hebrew, Persian, and Sanskrit. By embracing multiple cultures and the universal truth at the heart of all religions, these dances promote unity and neutralize destructive energies.

When people literally let go of focusing on external authorities, they become the actors. Whatever inspires them to dance en masse becomes obvious. Different than "crowd behavior," in which people are merely reacting to a stimulus, dancing together requires a more conscious intent. When I lead simple dances in large groups, I have people step back and forth, from side to side—that's all. Adding a peace chant raises the energy of a room and equalizes power over the greater body. We can each feel it when the crowd takes over. I am no longer "leading." When the time comes, I help draw the dance to a close, giving us the satisfaction of a clear ending. Experiences like this are vivid examples that dancing fosters a wider peace.

Dancing activates interpersonal peace. Daniel Goleman, in his book *Social Intelligence: The New Science of Social Relationships*, observes that strong, distressing states, like disgust, contempt, and explosive anger, are the "emotional equivalent of second-hand smoke that quietly damages the lungs of others who breathe in." He proposes, "The interpersonal equivalent of health boosting would be adding positive emotions to our surroundings."

A single male dancer on a hill at the Sasquatch Music Festival held in Washington State begins to dance to an irrepressible beat, overlaid with the words "I got to be unstoppable." In moments, another guy joins him and then another. It isn't clear what the tipping point for this collective dance is, but soon a hundred people are running to join the dance, wanting to get in on the action. It took just one guy to start this movement. An onlooker commented that those who want to change the world need his kind of exuberant joy. Dancing activates body-to-body communication and connection with each other. It *is* joyous peace.

Dancing educates communities in the art of peace. In an online document sponsored by the National Endowment for the Arts, called "The Arts in Peacemaking: A Guide to Integrating Conflict Resolution Education into Youth Arts Programs," Russell Brunson, Zephryn Conte, and Shelley Masar describe the work of Shirley Brice Heath, professor of English and education at Stanford University. Heath found that young people who were engaged in arts programs that met several times a week, for several hours a session over a year's time, had fewer brushes with the law. If they did end up in court, it was for less serious offenses. Heath also found that successful arts programs cultivated in the young people ways of being and habits of thinking essential in the arts, and that these habits carried over.

Moving in the Spirit, a youth troupe in Atlanta, is an example of urban youth creating dances together that require teamwork and discipline. They turned a year's study of racial tolerance into a dance. An Atlanta newspaper article described their "fleshy latticework" of "interlocking hands, wrists, and forearms" as more than the culmination of their work. It became their abiding symbol.

Dancing can celebrate diversity. Honoring different styles, body types, and strengths is both one of dance's stumbling blocks and one of its great potentials. We each have differences in temperament, blood type, vocational strengths, nutritional requirements, and exercise needs. Yet beyond these characteristics, beyond skin, race, religion, or class, we each embody the same four movement patterns: thrust, swing, shape, and hang. All are needed by those who want to dance with proficiency and beauty. Everything about the body points to both our individuality and our universality. When we dance for peace, we need both.

Diane Rawlinson, a Chicago high school dance teacher on a racially diverse campus, integrates principles of body, mind, heart, and spirit in her classes. She affirms the spirit, creativity, and common humanity of each student as valuable and teaches each of them to do the same. Representing financial, racial, and language groups from all over the map, her students' diversity is their key asset in their dance performances. Diane's alumni, having become part of something bigger, seek out and expect this same kind of diverse community in their world.

Dancing can redistribute and build power. When people dance together, the locus of authority shifts from something outside of individuals and into the group. Have you ever been in a group and finally felt free to do something crazier than normal? Groups empower us as long as we don't let go of our core values. Just as songs unite people, noncompetitive community dancing with a spiritual intention gives "power to the people." We see this in marches, parades, concerts, protests, and spectacles of religious people moving en masse in devotion. Dancing strengthens the collective web, and as an old African proverb says, "When spider webs unite, they can halt even a lion."

In Mumbai at the finale of an outdoor concert to promote global peace, a half-dozen dancers grabbed the hands of different audience members. Soon lines of people were snaking through the aisles as more and more people were caught up in the spirit of the moment. Though unplanned, it was incredibly moving to wind up in a great circle. We shouted, *"Namaste!"* (Peace!) and lifted our hands in the air. In this case, the saying "The more the merrier" became a demonstration of peace in action.

❖ ❖ ❖

A wonderful way to create a dance of peace is to take the elements of the hand-to-hand dance and move it from person to person in an informal, improvised way in this Dance of Peacemaking. You don't have to prescribe who will partner with whom. Allowing the possibility of brief contact with one or several people at a time, organic peaceful connections are never-ending.

Dance of Peacemaking

This dance is for a group. If there are nine or more people, cluster in smaller groups of three or four people.

~ Each person brings one hand to the center, making contact with the other hands.
~ Start by moving your hands, staying in contact, following the connection and flow.
~ Then open up some space between the hands, moving through and around each other.
~ Invite dancers to direct their hands outside the group, moving toward other dancers to make contact with a new person or group.
~ Dancing in connection, offer friendship and peace. As a connection evolves, eventually let go and move to new partners.

~ Once the community has practiced this interlocking contact, put on appropriate music and enjoy a dance of peacemaking.

~ In conclusion, if it seems appropriate for the energy of the group, join hands in a circle, take a deep breath, and offer words of gratitude and affirmation to each other.

❖ ❖ ❖

DANCING CULTURES OF PEACE

My friend Masankho is an ambassador for peace through song and dance. He does this in part because his grandmother told him to, but also because he knows that dance, drum, and song may be the only way to get out of the messes we get ourselves into. He travels the world showing youth and adults how to create cultures of peace. In *Conscious Dancer* magazine, he beautifully expressed the importance of his dancing village, saying, "The village was a place I could go to remember who I was. When I danced, I was connected to [the] source ... God, the ancestors. When I would dance, I knew even as a ten, or twelve, or fourteen-year-old that I was connecting with something else. You cannot stand on the shores of Lake Malawi, or under the bareback tree with fourteen drummers, somebody playing the top part, somebody playing the melody, somebody playing the lead, and not be transported to the center of spirit, to the very center of who you are."

I was fortunate to visit Masankho's ancestral home on the northern shores of Lake Malawi. When I arrived at the village with him and forty other travelers, I experienced the dancing village in action. It was dark, but the drums were playing even as we drove up. Disembarking from the bus, the village women danced their welcome to us on either side of the sidewalk. Rounding the corner of the house, twenty men danced, sang, and poured out their hospitality. Everyone wept. It felt like a true homecoming. Later, my seventeen-year-old daughter said she was never happier than when she was in Malawi.

Images of dancers in circles, lines, and spokes are recorded on the walls of cathedrals and temples, in books and paintings from earliest antiquity. We know they exist. But where do we find companies of dancing souls today, the kind who put sacred back into dance and take a path of love instead of competition? Do we have to go to Africa?

Perhaps our company is closer than we realize. Notice movement in your family, spiritual community, work group, club, civic organization, support group, team, artistic ensemble, or educational center. Can you sense when the group is thriving or losing energy, when they are on the move or stuck, creative or in a rut? How do they express themselves physically? Do they dance? If there is music playing, do you see toe tapping, grooving, and "getting down"? Does movement animate or irritate them? A group may not claim to practice dance, yet still embody the qualities of following, leading, and synchronicity we've been exploring. They may dance in unconscious ways. If so, celebrate this and join in the dance! If their bodies say, "No! Me, dance? Nah-uh, nope, we don't do that here," then let them be. Take it from me. You'll create more conflict than peace by trying to push people to move.

If you long for a dance community, you might want to search out a prominent movement system that certifies leaders who integrate dance and spirituality. (Some are listed in the Resources list at the end of the book.) If you can't find them in your area, check out the countless yoga or t'ai chi classes. These Eastern forms blend body consciousness, movement, breath, self-care, mindfulness, and spiritual awareness. They answer a need.

Or, you might consider forming a dance community of your own. Keep in mind that Divine Presence hums just fine to the tune of "wherever two or three are gathered" (Matthew 18:20, NRSV). Sacred movement collaborations can thrive with just you and one other person. Invite a friend to your house. Or encourage like-minded people to join you before or after a regularly scheduled gathering for an "experiment" with dance and prayer.

Some questions to consider when creating a dance community include: Will you gather more than one time? Will you use dance as meditation? Will there be space for more extroverted, interactive movement to celebrate and have fun? Will you focus on a theme? Do you want to dance on behalf of others? Will you use a routine ritual for the process each time? How will you start and end?

From years of leading dance communities, I've discovered some useful principles to keep in mind. Your basic intentions and actions will convey the emotional and spiritual quality of the group you are forming. I appreciate the way Carolyn invites me into her bottomless well of spirit and healing. Phil is poised; his charisma is in his joy in making things. Being in Carla's presence is like going to church. When Rod leads, I feel creatively unzipped: God is wild and untamable.

In every case, these spiritual leaders pay attention to the following four basic areas: hospitality and invitation, focus and attention, simplicity and brevity, and choosing the forms of interaction.

HOSPITALITY AND INVITATION

Hospitality is key to the dance of life. Giving people freedom to both participate and witness each other, as needed, makes room for a wide breadth of individual circumstance and energies. Nanette Sawyer, in her book *Hospitality—The Sacred Art: Discovering the Hidden Power of Invitation and Welcome* (Skylight Paths), sees hospitality literally embodied in "postures": the posture of invitation, which is born of receptivity; the posture of welcome, which is born of reverence; and the posture of nurture, which is born of generosity.

In my dance studio, when friends enter the space, I let them know that I see them. If possible, I hug or greet them. If they lie down on the floor, I honor their energy. Sometimes, that's where we start. I seek to preserve the individual space of group members. Many people need time alone. I trust them to their process as I endeavor to create space rather than fill it with me and my teaching.

Another way I create hospitality is to join the dance rather than stand back. Participating as a leader is one way I let others know that I am not there to judge or try to control people. I am dancing my own spiritual practice.

How might you invite people to start moving? In a small group I simply call people to a circle. Sometimes I choose a specific prayer or song to begin a session. When I put on music, I invite everyone to take a deep breath. We shake out our limbs and proceed with a simple, familiar warm-up. Rather than impose my words for God, I stay open to many ways of naming Divinity, entrusting a wide range of music, space, song, and dance to lead us to common sacred ground.

As I lead, it is important not to focus too much on any one individual's expression or needs. Any attempts at directing people's emotions can make them feel more vulnerable. As a leader of sacred practices, I leave specific emotional outcomes to God. Dance as a sacred practice is not therapy. Unless specific healing is requested or offered, I see dancing as an open process for moving our prayers.

An excellent way to invite people to nurture prayer experiences through movement is to let them rest in stillness after periods of dancing. In that holy of holies, silence, people can find receptive space to offer prayers and savor their experience. Hospitality to the sacred in such a way is a rare gift.

FOCUS AND INTENTION

Creating sacred space begins with an intention. I appreciate the basic, elegant outline suggested by Malidoma Some's African wisdom. In his book *The Healing Wisdom of Africa*, he says that the first part in creating a ritual is to *clarify your intention*. The second part is to *make a shrine, altar, or focus for your intention*. The third is to *interact with the shrine/intention*. An intention can be extremely basic. It can be something as simple as "I want to move with the Divine in others and myself."

Once you discern an intention, it can help to create a visual focus. Images move us to see beyond ourselves. Some dance communities collectively improvise an altar at the beginning of a session. A focus can be as simple as lighting a candle, making a circle, or sitting close together, letting your feet intermingle—a powerful image for isolated people. Brief words and phrases, like "My body is a temple," also focus and enshrine a moment of prayer.

SIMPLICITY AND BREVITY

When shaping a sacred dance practice, keep it simple. Remember that spirituality is experiential, physical, and mysterious. The Divine will inevitably surprise you if you let go of the compulsion to take charge of everything. I believe that's the point: We need to be open to Spirit. Don't overcomplicate it with too many steps, ideas, or plans. At the same time, participants need enough structure and enough of a plan so they can relax. They need a map. Many enjoy having a guide to help release them from worrying about "figuring" it all out.

Don't rush from form to form. You can repeat practices over and over with slight variations, like a change in music. Though the content of our lives changes, the forms we use needn't vary that much. You might choose several forms that you enjoy and use them again and again. When you are ready for a challenge or a new idea, it will present itself.

Keep experiences brief when people are new to movement. Two to five minutes of dance is plenty. Once folks are comfortable, you can extend dancing to the length of a sitting meditation practice (from five to twenty-five minutes). For the kinesthetically inclined, it is luxurious to have a rare twenty minutes of uninterrupted moving meditation. Being allowed to pray in our "first language" can quickly quiet our mind. On the other hand, freeform dancing can feel pointless, monotonous, or even threatening to some. Notice if you or others feel drained. Calculate the length of time according to your group's needs.

FORMS OF INTERACTION

There are many ways to interact with a prayer intention. You can "Dance on Behalf Of" someone (see page 101), do a hand-to-hand dance for restoring connections (see page 135), a one-minute Dance of Exformation (see page 87), Walk, Stop, and Run to connect with community (see page 155), or some other simple form. (See the Index of Movement Practices at the back of the book.) You might want to offer an open period where everyone who is so moved can dance side by side in response to a common need without worrying about coordinating with one another. When the focus of the group is challenging, like when people are dealing with death and loss, keep in mind that simpler, less complicated dance forms are best.

As a group becomes comfortable with and knowledgeable about each other, you may discover that certain individuals enjoy singing, playing an instrument, or writing poetry. You could invite them to sing a song, provide an accompaniment, or share a poem while others dance alone or hand to hand. The possibilities for prayerful sharing will evolve the more confident and trusting a group becomes.

❖ ❖ ❖

In closing, I want to offer you a simple template for body prayer that is communal, body-based, and honors needs through participation, witnessing, and rest. The emphasis is on deepening sacred experiences in a ritual that lasts anywhere from ten to thirty minutes or more.

Communal Body Prayer

GATHERING MEMBERS:

~ Gather in a circle with silence, verbal prayer, or song.

~ To warm up, take some deep breaths and sigh. Shake out your arms, legs, and middle.

~ Start with swinging, sweeping motions to clear unwanted energies. Include flinging and thrusting movements.

~ Shift to slow, smooth "fake t'ai chi" moves to gather life energy back from the projects, people, places, and things that people are involved in.

~ As people feel grounded (after five to seven minutes), enjoy a minute of silence and conclude with a deep breath.

OFFERING A CONCERN OR A GIFT:

~ Choose a word, theme, image, concern, text, artwork, story, or music as a focus.

RESPONSE:

~ Respond to whatever is offered by inviting an individual, pairs, or the group to dance with a suggested form. For ideas on specific movements, see the Index of Movement Practices and the Resources list at the back of the book.

~ Remind people of their role as sacred witnesses. If need be, support them to find their easy focus, and affirm their ability to look for the good.

BLESSING OF PEACE:

~ To conclude, you could do a Dance of Peacemaking with hand-to-hand contact.

~ End a circle dance by having people join hands and hum while group members speak or sing phrases of gratitude. Or, you could simply join hands in stillness.

RELEASE:

~ To release the group, invite everyone to reach into the center and send the abundant, prayerful connection out into the world to serve wherever it is needed.

❖ ❖ ❖

In Keri Hulme's novel *The Bone People*, she writes, "Even paired, any pairing, they would have been nothing more than people by themselves. But all together, they have become the heart and muscles and mind of something perilous and new, something strange and growing and great. Together, all together, they are the instruments of change." I believe that when we dance with others, we transform. Movement enables our highest good and mysteriously makes God known even when we can't say exactly who or what God is.

To take up dance as a spiritual practice is to practice resurrection. Rising up with body and soul, reincarnating ourselves in beautiful ways, is what life, love, and the glory of God want for us. Lee Ann Womak's famous song beseeches, "When you get the choice to sit it out or dance, I hope you dance." Even when it feels as though the last thing you want to do is move, if you take your prayers and let them move to the music in your body, miracles can occur, peace will come. A new heaven and a new earth are quite literally "at hand."

RESOURCES

AUTHENTIC MOVEMENT

WWW.AUTHENTICMOVEMENT-USA.COM

Authentic Movement is a self-directed, therapeutic form of movement. Individuals discover movement pathways that offer a bridge between conscious and unconscious ways of knowing. With a witness, a dancer closes her eyes and listens inwardly to find movement arising from hidden prompting. As the invisible becomes visible, the witness participates with the dancer. Founder Mary Starks Whitehouse believed, "The body is the physical aspect of the personality and movement is the personality made visible." This discipline is grounded in developmental psychology, somatic epistemology, Jungian thought, dance ethnology, and mystical studies.

BIODANZA (DANCE OF LIFE)

WWW.BIODANZA.US

Biodanza (Dance of Life) is an expressive arts system that incorporates music, movement, and authentic relationships with self, others, and the world to support health, joy, and being fully alive. The practice is conducted through two-hour weekly classes and weekend workshops and is based on anthropological studies of dance and traditional rituals of the celebration of life. Biodanza stimulates community, awakens a consciousness of universal solidarity, helps participants to recover their joy and vitality, and celebrates the sacredness of life. It has evolved over four decades in Latin America and Europe under the vision of founder Rolando Toro Araneda.

CONTACT IMPROVISATION

WWW.CONTACTIMPROV.NET

Contact Improvisation is a partner dance form based on touch, momentum, shared weight, and following a shared point of contact. Founder Steve Paxton drew from his background as a modern dancer and his studies in aikido. Contact Improvisation tends to bring together open-minded, openhearted people from around the world. Dance for pleasure and health, which is full of art, improvisation, happiness, and spontaneous play with space, defines this form. CI leader Mark Moti Zemelman reveals aspects of the spirituality found in this dance practice, saying, "Contact Improvisation is an honoring of every moment…. In this form one learns to stay in integrity with each choice, never forcing, never rushing. When body, mind, and spirit are united in their instinctive wisdom, one finds oneself at home in every moment expressing one's true nature."

DANCE THERAPY

WWW.ADTA.ORG

According to the American Dance Therapy Association, "Dance/movement therapy is the psychotherapeutic use of movement as a process which furthers the emotional, cognitive, social and physical integration of the individual." Members of the Academy of Dance Therapists Registered (ADTR), who are qualified to engage in private practice, are listed in the members' directory on the American Dance Association website.

5RHYTHMS

WWW.GABRIELLEROTH.COM

5Rhythms is a movement meditation practice, created by Gabrielle Roth, which focuses on "putting our body in motion in order to still the mind and allow the student to connect to the spiritual. The five rhythms [in order] are: flowing, staccato, chaos, lyrical, and stillness." Dancing in a sequence known as a "wave," students often refer to this as a way to "sweat your prayers," or a mix of "Sunday morning gospel service, Friday night dance club, and Saturday morning aerobics class." Participants find it helps them to "deepen understanding of natural truth, the nature of humanity, and 'ground' the mind [and spirit] by connecting back to the body."

INTERNATIONAL NETWORK FOR THE DANCES OF UNIVERSAL PEACE

WWW.DANCESOFUNIVERSALPEACE.ORG

The International Network for the Dances of Universal Peace links dance circles around the world through Peaceworks Inc., the supporting not-for-profit organization. Founded by Samuel Lewis, the dances inspired a registry of dance leaders, networkers, and a Mentor Teachers Guild, who share movements and songs drawn from over five hundred dances around the world. Dancers focus on peace and harmony, creating a sense of solidarity and community while celebrating the underlying unity of all spiritual traditions.

InterPlay
WWW.INTERPLAY.ORG

InterPlay groups include bodyspirit playgroups, Untensive Retreats, and life practice programs offered in the United States, Australia, India, Europe, and Brazil. Founded in 1989 under the umbrella of Body Wisdom, Inc. by Phil Porter and Cynthia Winton-Henry, InterPlay is an active, creative approach to unlocking the wisdom of the body. Sharing the spirited joy that "any body can have" when we improvise move, play, and create, InterPlay helps people integrate elements of art, spirituality, social consciousness, community development, and healing practices. Certified teachers steeped in the holistic philosophy apply InterPlay's principles to benefit both individuals and groups who seek an incremental, accessible toolkit for increasing vital, soulful connections.

Moving Arts Network and *Conscious Dancer* Magazine: Movement for a Better World
WWW.CONSCIOUSDANCER.COM

This online directory, monthly e-zine, and quarterly magazine connect the growing conscious dance community—one more sign that people are returning to dance as a sacred art. Started by Mark Metz and Aspen Madrone in 2007 in the San Francisco Bay Area, this hub of the moving arts community "celebrates transformative dance, mind-body fitness, and energy movement arts" and shares what is happening in the field.

Nia
WWW.NIANOW.COM

Nia is taught internationally as "movement-medicine for the body and soul." Created by Debbie and Carlos Rosas to simultaneously address body, mind, emotions, and spirit by putting them on the "same page" using music, movement, and personal expression, Nia blends nine movement forms taken from the martial arts (t'ai chi, tae kwon do, and aikido); the dance arts (jazz dance, modern dance, and Duncan dancing); and the healing arts (yoga, Alexander technique, and the teachings of Moshe Feldenkrais). Nia is practiced barefoot to music and is "adaptable and safe for any fitness level, from stiff beginners to highly fit athletes." While delivering whole-body conditioning, Nia is "based on creating a loving relationship with the body and following the Body's Way—the innate intelligence of the body."

SACRED DANCE GUILD
WWW.SACREDDANCEGUILD.ORG

The Sacred Dance Guild is an international, multicultural, interfaith, nonprofit organization that offers festivals, regional workshops, and information to enrich those of all ages, backgrounds, and abilities. Its mission is "to promote sacred dance as prayer, and as a means of spiritual growth, connection to the Divine, and integration of mind, body, and spirit."

TAMALPA LIFE/ART PROCESS
WWW.TAMALPA.ORG

Tamalpa Life/Art Process, founded by Anna Halprin and Daria Halprin, is a nonprofit, movement-based, expressive arts organization. Tamalpa Institute is their internationally recognized school for dance/movement-based expressive arts education and therapy. The tools of the life/art process include movement/dance, voice/sound, drawing, dialogue, improvisation, performance, and reflection. Taught internationally, this approach has led to innovative performance work around the world for over fifty years. The founders believe that spirituality is enhanced when people are able to express themselves with physical, emotional, and mental awareness and creativity.

SUGGESTIONS FOR

FURTHER READING

Adams, Doug. *Congregational Dancing in Christian Worship.* Austin, Tex.: Sharing, 1984.

————, ed. *Dancing Christmas Carols.* San Jose, Calif.: Resource Publications, 1978.

————, and Diane Apostolos-Cappadona, eds. *Dance as Religious Studies.* San Jose, Calif.: Resource Publications, 2001.

Adyashanti. *Emptiness Dancing.* Boulder, Colo.: Sounds True, 2006.

Albright, Ann Cooper, and David Gere, eds. *Taken by Surprise: A Dance Improvisation Reader.* Middletown, Conn.: Wesleyan University Press, 2003.

Blom, Lynne Anne, and L. Tarin Chaplin. *The Moment of Movement: Dance Improvisation.* Hampshire, UK: Dance Books, 2008.

Buber, Martin. *I and Thou.* Translated by Walter Kaufmann. New York: Free Press, 1971.

Carter, Aimée. "The Startling Truth about Your Own Dark Side," *New Spirit Journal*, April 2009, 4.

Collins, Sheila K. *Stillpoint—The Dance of Selfcaring, Selfhealing: A Playbook for People Who Do Caring Work.* Fort Worth, Tex.: TLC Productions, 1992.

Csikszentmihalyi, Mihaly. *Flow: The Psychology of Optimal Experience.* New York: Harper Perennial Modern Classics, 2008.

DeSola, Carla. *Peace Rites.* Washington, D.C.: Pastoral Press, 1993.

————, and Doug Adams. *The Spirit Moves: Handbook of Dance and Prayer.* Austin, Tex.: Sharing, 1986.

Ehrenreich, Barbara. *Dancing in the Streets: A History of Collective Joy.* New York: Metropolitan, 2007.

Falkowski, Pamela Jean. "My Body, My Prayer—Celebrating Embodied Spirituality and Sexuality in a Christian Tradition: A

Course for Spiritual Directors." DMin diss., Pacific School of Religion, 2002.

Fischer, John. *Real Christians Don't Dance!* Minneapolis, Minn.: Bethany House, 1994.

Fox, Matthew. *Original Blessing: A Primer in Creation Spirituality Presented in Four Paths, Twenty-Six Themes, and Two Questions.* New York: Tarcher/Putnam, 2000.

Friedman, Lenore, and Susan Moon, eds. *Being Bodies: Buddhist Women on the Paradox of Embodiment.* Boston: Shambhala, 1997.

Fulghum, Robert. *All I Really Need to Know I Learned in Kindergarten.* 15th ed. New York: Ballantine Books, 2004.

Galanter, Mark. *Spirituality and the Healthy Mind: Science, Therapy, and the Need for Personal Meaning.* New York: Oxford University Press, 2005.

Gardner, Howard. *Frames of Mind: The Theory of Multiple Intelligences.* New York: Basic, 1993.

Gilbert, Anne Green. *Creative Dance for All Ages: A Conceptual Approach.* Reston, Va.: American Alliance for Health, Physical Education, Recreation, and Dance, 1992.

Goleman, Daniel. *Social Intelligence: The New Science of Human Relationships.* New York: Bantam, 2007.

Gordon, James S. *Unstuck: Your Guide to the Seven-Stage Journey Out of Depression.* New York: Penguin, 2009.

Green, Barry. *Bringing Music to Life.* Chicago: GIA Publications, 2009.

Halprin, Daria. *The Expressive Body in Life, Art and Therapy: Working with Movement, Metaphor and Meaning.* New York: Jessica Kingsley, 2008.

Hammerschlag, Carl A. *The Dancing Healers: A Doctor's Journey of Healing with Native Americans.* New York: HarperCollins, 1998.

Hays, Edward M. *Pray All Ways: A Book for Daily Worship Using All Your Senses.* Easton, Kans.: Forest of Peace, 1981.

Highwater, Jamake. *Dance: Rituals of Experience.* New York: Oxford University Press, 1996.

Hodgson, John. *Mastering Movement: The Life and Work of Rudolf Laban.* New York: Routledge, 2001.

Horwitz, Claudia. *The Spiritual Activist: Practices to Transform Your Life, Your Work, and Your World.* New York: Penguin, 2002.

Hume, Keri. *The Bone People.* Baton Rouge: Louisiana State University Press, 2005.

Humphrey, Doris. *The Art of Making Dances.* Princeton, N.J.: Princeton Book Co., 1991.

Ingerman, Sandra. *Soul Retrieval: Mending the Fragmented Self.* San Francisco: HarperOne, 2006.

Jones, Adele Decker. "A Step Toward Demonstrating a Model for the Therapeutic Use of Creative/Expression Body Movements in Pastoral Counseling and Psychotherapy." DMin diss., Garrett-Evangelical Theological Seminary and Seabury-Western Theological Seminary, 1997.

Kabat-Zinn, Jon. *Full Catastrophe Living: Using the Wisdom of Your Body and Mind to Face Stress, Pain, and Illness.* New York: Delta, 1990.

Keeney, Bradford. *Bushman Shaman: Awakening the Spirit through Ecstatic Dance.* Rochester, Vt.: Destiny, 2004.

———. *Shaking Medicine: The Healing Power of Ecstatic Movement.* Rochester, Vt.: 2007.

King, Ruth. *Healing Rage: Women Making Inner Peace Possible.* New York: Penguin/Gotham, 2008.

Lakoff, George, and Mark Johnson. *Philosophy in the Flesh: The Embodied Mind and Its Challenge to Western Thought.* New York: Basic, 1999.

Langer, Suzanne K. *Feeling and Form.* New York: Prentice Hall, 1977.

Lewis, C. S. *Perelandra.* New York: Scribner, 2003.

Lindbergh, Anne Morrow. *Gift from the Sea.* New York: Pantheon, 1991.

Lowen, Alexander. *Joy: The Surrender to the Body and to Life.* New York: Penguin, 1995.

MacBeth, Sybil. *Praying in Color: Drawing a New Path to God.* Active Prayer series. Brewster, Mass.: Paraclete Press, 2007.

Martland, Thomas R. *Religion as Art: An Interpretation.* Albany, N.Y.: State University of New York Press, 1981.

McFague, Sallie. *The Body of God: An Ecological Theology.* Minneapolis, Minn.: Augsburg Fortress, 1993.

McFee, Marcia. "Primal Patterns: Ritual Dynamics, Ritual Resonance, Polyrhythmic Strategies and the Formation of Christian Disciples." PhD diss., Graduate Theological Union, 2005.

Miles, Margaret Ruth. *Augustine on the Body*. American Academy of Religion Dissertation series, no. 31. Missoula, Mont.: Scholars Press, 1979.

Miller, Robert, ed. *The Complete Gospels: Annotated Scholars Version*. 2nd ed. Santa Rose, Calif.: Polebridge Press, 1994.

Mindell, Arnold. *The Shaman's Body: A New Shamanism for Transforming Health, Relationships, and the Community*. San Francisco, Calif.: HarperOne, 1993.

Moltmann-Wendel, Elizabeth. *I Am My Body: A Theology of Embodiment*. New York: Continuum, 1995.

Morrill, Bruce T., ed. *Bodies of Worship: Explorations in Theory and Practice*. Collegeville, Minn.: Liturgical Press, 1999.

Morrison, Dorothy, and Kristen Madden. *Dancing the Goddess Incarnate: Living the Magic of Maiden, Mother and Crone*. Woodbury, Minn.: Llewellyn, 2006.

Murphy, Michael. *The Future of the Body: Explorations into the Further Evolution of Human Nature*. New York: Tarcher/Putnam, 1993.

Nachmanovitch, Stephen. *Free Play: Improvisation in Life and Art*. New York: Tarcher/Putnam, 1991.

Narby, Jeremy. *The Cosmic Serpent: DNA and the Origins of Knowledge*. New York: Tarcher/Putnam, 1999.

Nelson, James B. *Body Theology*. Louisville, Ky.: Westminster/John Knox Press, 1992.

Nhat Hanh, Thich. *Breathe, You Are Alive!—The Sutra on the Full Awareness of Breathing*. Berkeley, Calif.: Parallax Press, 2008.

———. *The Long Road Turns to Joy: A Guide to Walking Meditation*. Berkeley, Calif.: Parallax Press, 1996.

Nouwen, Henri J. M. *Reaching Out: The Three Movements of the Spiritual Life*. New York: Image, 1986.

O'Murchu, Diarmuid. *Quantum Theology: Spiritual Implications of the New Physics*. New York: Crossroad, 2004.

Pennebaker, James W. *Opening Up: The Healing Power of Expressing Emotions*. New York: Guilford, 1997.

Pink, Daniel H. *A Whole New Mind: Why Right-Brainers Will Rule the Future*. New York: Riverhead, 2008.

Plaizier, Tom. *Creativity, Fun and Play—God's Gifts for the Ministry of the Local Congregation*. DMin diss., San Francisco Theological Seminary, 1977.

Porter, Phil. *Having It All: Body, Mind, Heart and Spirit Together Again at Last.* Oakland, Calif.: Wing It! Press, 1997.

———. *The Slightly Mad Rantings of a Body Intellectual, Part One.* Oakland, Calif.: Wing It! Press, 2008.

———. *The Wisdom of the Body: The InterPlay Philosophy and Technique.* Oakland, Calif.: Wing It! Press, 1995.

Redmond, Layne. *When the Drummers Were Women: A Spiritual History of Rhythm.* New York: Three Rivers, 1997.

Richo, David. *Shadow Dance: Liberating the Power and Creativity of Your Dark Side.* Boston: Shambhala, 1999.

Rock, Judith. *Theology in the Shape of Dance: Using Dance in Worship and Theological Process.* Austin, Tex.: Sharing, 1978.

———, and Norman Mealy. *Performer as Priest and Prophet: Restoring the Intuitive in Worship through Music and Dance.* San Francisco: HarperCollins, 1988.

Rogers, Natalie. *The Creative Connection: Expressive Arts as Healing.* Ross-on-Wye, UK: PCCS, 2000.

Sankaran, Rajan. *The Other Song: Discovering Your Parallel Self.* Mumbai: Homeopathic Medical Publishers, 2008.

Sawyer, Nanette. *Hospitality—The Sacred Art: Discovering the Hidden Spiritual Power of Invitation and Welcome.* Woodstock, Vt.: SkyLight Paths, 2007.

Snowber, Celeste. *Embodied Prayer: Towards Wholeness of Body, Mind, Soul.* Kelowna, B.C.: Northstone, 2004.

Somé, Malidoma Patrice. *The Healing Wisdom of Africa: Finding Life Purpose through Nature, Ritual, and Community.* New York: Tarcher/Putnam, 1999.

St. Denis, Ruth. *Ruth St. Denis, An Unfinished Life: An Autobiography.* Dance Horizons series 30. Brooklyn, N.Y.: Dance Horizons, 1969.

———. *Wisdom Comes Dancing: Selected Writings of Ruth St. Denis on Dance, Spirituality, and the Body.* Seattle: Peaceworks, 1997.

Stromsted, Tina. "Re-Inhabiting the Female Body: Authentic Movement as a Gateway to Transformation." PhD diss., University of Oregon, 1999.

Sweeney, Jon M. *Praying with Our Hands: 21 Practices of Embodied Prayer from the World's Spiritual Traditions.* Woodstock, Vt.: SkyLight Paths, 2000.

Tucker, JoAnne, and Susan Freeman. *Torah in Motion: Creating Dance Midrash.* New York: e-reads.com, 1999.

Van der Kolk, Bessel A. "Developmental Trauma Disorder: A More Specific Diagnosis than Posttraumatic Stress Disorder Should Be Considered for Children with Complex Trauma Histories." *Psychiatric Annals* 35, no. 5 (2005): 401–409.

———. "In Terror's Grip: Healing the Ravages of Trauma." *Cerebrum* 4 (Winter 2002): 34–50.

Van der Leeuw, Gerardus. *Sacred and Profane Beauty: The Holy in Art.* American Academy of Religion Texts and Translations series. New York: Oxford University Press, 2006.

Vennard, Jane E. *Praying with Body and Soul: A Way to Intimacy with God.* Minneapolis, Minn.: Augsburg Fortress, 1998.

Wheatley, Margaret J., and Myron Kellner-Rogers. *A Simpler Way.* San Francisco: Berrett-Koehler, 1998.

Whitelaw, Ginny, and Betsy Wetzig. *Move to Greatness: Focusing the Four Essential Energies of a Whole and Balanced Leader.* Boston: Nicholas Brealey, 2008.

Winton-Henry, Cynthia. *Body and Soul: Excursions in the Realm of Physicality and Spirituality.* Oakland, Calif.: Wing It!, 1993.

———. *Chasing the Dance of Life: A Faith Journey.* Berkeley, Calif.: Apocryphile, 2009.

———. *What the Body Wants.* Kelowna, BC: Northstone, 2004.

Wuellner, Flora Slosson. *Prayer and Our Bodies.* Nashville, Tenn.: Upper Room, 1987.

Wuthnow, Robert. *All in Sync: How Music and Art Are Revitalizing American Religion.* Berkeley, Calif.: University of California Press, 2006.

INDEX OF MOVEMENT PRACTICES

GRATITUDE

How grateful I am for the rising tide of dancers, scholars, scientists, and spiritual seekers who buoy and inspire dance as a spiritual practice. Barbara Ehrenreich, your book *Dancing in the Streets: A History of Collective Joy* answers the question "What happened to dance, to the festival?" Thank you! Malidoma Some, your spirit in *The Healing Wisdom of Africa: Finding Life Purpose through Art, Nature, Ritual, and Community* blesses and affirms all who claim the arts and artists in spiritual life. Thank you! Betsy Wetzig and Ginny Whitelaw, friends and authors of *Move to Greatness: Focusing the Four Balances Energies of a Whole and Balanced Life*, you gave decades to the meaning of the four movement patterns for life. What a breakthrough! Thank you!

I carry these books into my conversations everywhere. But inside the pockets of my cells, I carry conversations with you, Phil Porter, friend, guide, collaborator, and powerhouse of InterPlayful wisdom. I thank God for you.

To my InterPlay community in North America, Australia, India, and Europe, and to the Sacred Dance Guild, know that I was thinking of you as I wrote these words, attempting to say something of what it has meant to us to rediscover the wisdom of the body and come to a place so full of grace. Together, we are lucky. I hope this book will support our dream of a world dancing in peace.

Pacific School of Religion and Doug Adams, you gave me a place to develop and teach dance as a spiritual practice. To my twenty years of students who moved, wrote, and taught me the beauty and challenge of embodying life's truths, I bow to you in humble appreciation.

Marcia Broucek, my SkyLight Paths editor, having never met body to body, I am moved by your care for the words and

ideas in this book. Thank you for reading with the eyes of someone new to dancing. This refreshed me. Both the book and my
work benefited deeply. Thank you.

My daughter, Katie, this book is part of my legacy to you.
Whether or not you consider dance as part of your spiritual practice, you and I both know that welcoming others through music
and dance makes a difference. I dance so that you might dance as
well.

Last to be mentioned, but first in my heart, Stephen, thank
you for being my beloved and for giving me the space, time, and
nourishment to follow my path. I love you.

Sacred Texts—cont.

CHRISTIANITY

The End of Days: Essential Selections from Apocalyptic Texts—Annotated & Explained *Annotation by Robert G. Clouse*
Helps you understand the complex Christian visions of the end of the world.
5½ x 8½, 224 pp, Quality PB, 978-1-59473-170-9 **$16.99**

The Hidden Gospel of Matthew: Annotated & Explained
Translation & Annotation by Ron Miller
Takes you deep into the text cherished around the world to discover the words and events that have the strongest connection to the historical Jesus.
5½ x 8½, 272 pp, Quality PB, 978-1-59473-038-2 **$16.99**

The Infancy Gospels of Jesus: Apocryphal Tales from the Childhoods of Mary and Jesus—Annotated & Explained *Stevan Davies; Foreword by A. Edward Siecienski*
A startling presentation of the early lives of Mary, Jesus, and other biblical figures that will amuse and surprise you. 5½ x 8½, 176 pp, Quality PB Original, 978-1-59473-258-4 **$16.99**

The Lost Sayings of Jesus: Teachings from Ancient Christian, Jewish, Gnostic and Islamic Sources—Annotated & Explained
Translation & Annotation by Andrew Phillip Smith; Foreword by Stephan A. Hoeller
This collection of more than three hundred sayings depicts Jesus as a Wisdom teacher who speaks to people of all faiths as a mystic and spiritual master.
5½ x 8½, 240 pp, Quality PB, 978-1-59473-172-3 **$16.99**

Philokalia: The Eastern Christian Spiritual Texts—Selections Annotated & Explained
Annotation by Allyne Smith; Translation by G. E. H. Palmer, Phillip Sherrard and Bishop Kallistos Ware
The first approachable introduction to the wisdom of the Philokalia, which is the classic text of Eastern Christian spirituality. 5½ x 8½, 240 pp, Quality PB, 978-1-59473-103-7 **$16.99**

The Sacred Writings of Paul: Selections Annotated & Explained
Translation & Annotation by Ron Miller
Explores the apostle Paul's core message of spiritual equality, freedom and joy.
5½ x 8½, 224 pp, Quality PB, 978-1-59473-213-3 **$16.99**

Sex Texts from the Bible: Selections Annotated & Explained
Translation & Annotation by Teresa J. Hornsby; Foreword by Amy-Jill Levine
Offers surprising insight into our modern sexual lives.
5½ x 8½, 208 pp, Quality PB, 978-1-59473-217-1 **$16.99**

Spiritual Writings on Mary: Annotated & Explained
Annotation by Mary Ford-Grabowsky; Foreword by Andrew Harvey
Examines the role of Mary, the mother of Jesus, as a source of inspiration in history and in life today. 5½ x 8½, 288 pp, Quality PB, 978-1-59473-001-6 **$16.99**

The Way of a Pilgrim: The Jesus Prayer Journey—Annotated & Explained
Translation & Annotation by Gleb Pokrovsky; Foreword by Andrew Harvey
This classic of Russian spirituality is the delightful account of one man who sets out to learn the prayer of the heart, also known as the "Jesus prayer."
5½ x 8½, 160 pp, Illus., Quality PB, 978-1-893361-31-7 **$14.95**

JUDAISM

The Divine Feminine in Biblical Wisdom Literature
Selections Annotated & Explained
Translation & Annotation by Rabbi Rami Shapiro; Foreword by Rev. Cynthia Bourgeault, PhD
Uses the Hebrew books of Psalms, Proverbs, Song of Songs, Ecclesiastes and Job, Wisdom literature and the Wisdom of Solomon to clarify who Wisdom is.
5½ x 8½, 240 pp, Quality PB, 978-1-59473-109-0 **$16.99**

Ethics of the Sages: *Pirke Avot*—Annotated & Explained
Translation & Annotation by Rabbi Rami Shapiro
Clarifies the ethical teachings of the early Rabbis. 5½ x 8½, 192 pp, Quality PB, 978-1-59473-207-2 **$16.99**

Children's Spirituality

Adam and Eve's First Sunset: God's New Day
by Sandy Eisenberg Sasso; Full-color illus. by Joani Keller Rothenberg 9 x 12, 32 pp, Full-color illus.,
HC, 978-1-58023-177-0 **$17.95** *For ages 4 & up (A book from Jewish Lights, SkyLight Paths' sister imprint)*

Because Nothing Looks Like God
by Lawrence and Karen Kushner; Full-color illus. by Dawn W. Majewski
Real-life examples of happiness and sadness introduce children to the possibilities of
spiritual life. 11 x 8½, 32 pp, HC, Full-color illus., 978-1-58023-092-6 **$17.99**
For ages 4 & up (A book from Jewish Lights, SkyLight Paths' sister imprint)
Also available: **Teacher's Guide,** 8½ x 11, 22 pp, PB, 978-1-58023-140-4 **$6.95** *For ages 5–8*

But God Remembered: Stories of Women from Creation to the
Promised Land *by Sandy Eisenberg Sasso; Full-color illus. by Bethanne Andersen*
A fascinating collection of four different stories of women only briefly mentioned in
biblical tradition and religious texts.
9 x 12, 32 pp, Full-color illus., Quality PB, 978-1-58023-372-9 **$12.99**; HC, 978-1-879045-43-9
$16.95
For ages 8 & up (A book from Jewish Lights, SkyLight Paths' sister imprint)

Cain & Abel: Finding the Fruits of Peace
by Sandy Eisenberg Sasso; Full-color illus. by Joani Keller Rothenberg
A sensitive recasting of the ancient tale shows we have the power to deal with anger in positive
ways. "Editor's Choice"—American Library Association's *Booklist*
9 x 12, 32 pp, HC, Full-color illus., 978-1-58023-123-7 **$16.95** *For ages 5 & up (A book from Jewish Lights,
SkyLight Paths' sister imprint)*

Does God Hear My Prayer?
by August Gold; Full-color photos by Diane Hardy Waller
Introduces preschoolers and young readers to prayer and how it helps them express their own
emotions. 10 x 8½, 32 pp, Quality PB, Full-color photo illus., 978-1-59473-102-0 **$8.99**

The 11th Commandment: Wisdom from Our Children *by The Children of America*
"If there were an Eleventh Commandment, what would it be?" Children of many religious
denominations across America answer this question—in their own drawings and words. "A
rare book of spiritual celebration for all people, of all ages, for all time." —*Bookviews*
8 x 10, 48 pp, HC, Full-color illus., 978-1-879045-46-0 **$16.95**
For all ages (A book from Jewish Lights, SkyLight Paths' sister imprint)

For Heaven's Sake *by Sandy Eisenberg Sasso; Full-color illus. by Kathryn Kunz Finney*
What heaven is and where to find it. 9 x 12, 32 pp, HC, Full-color illus., 978-1-58023-054-4 **$16.95**
For ages 4 & up (A book from Jewish Lights, SkyLight Paths' sister imprint)

God in Between *by Sandy Eisenberg Sasso; Full-color illus. by Sally Sweetland*
A magical, mythical tale that teaches that God can be found where we are.
9 x 12, 32 pp, HC, Full-color illus., 978-1-879045-86-6 **$16.95** *For ages 4 & up (A book from Jewish
Lights, SkyLight Paths' sister imprint)*

God's Paintbrush: Special 10th Anniversary Edition
Invites children of all faiths and backgrounds to encounter God through moments in their
own lives. 11 x 8½, 32 pp, Full-color illus., HC, 978-1-58023-195-4 **$17.95** *For ages 4 & up*
Also available: **I Am God's Paintbrush** (A Board Book)
by Sandy Eisenberg Sasso; Full-color illus. by Annette Compton
5 x 5, 24 pp, Board Book, Full-color illus., 978-1-59473-265-2 **$7.99** *For ages 0–4*
Also available: **God's Paintbrush Teacher's Guide** 8½ x 11, 32 pp, PB, 978-1-879045-57-6 **$8.95**
God's Paintbrush Celebration Kit
A Spiritual Activity Kit for Teachers and Students of All Faiths, All Backgrounds
Additional activity sheets available:
8-Student Activity Sheet Pack (40 sheets/5 sessions), 978-1-58023-058-2 **$19.95**
Single-Student Activity Sheet Pack (5 sessions), 978-1-58023-059-9 **$3.95**

Children's Spirituality

Remembering My Grandparent: A Kid's Own Grief Workbook in the Christian Tradition *by Nechama Liss-Levinson, PhD, and Rev. Molly Phinney Baskette, MDiv* 8 x 10, 48 pp, 2-color text, HC, 978-1-59473-212-6 **$16.99** *For ages 7–13*

Does God Ever Sleep? *by Joan Sauro, CSJ; Full-color photos*
A charming nighttime reminder that God is always present in our lives.
10 x 8½, 32 pp, Quality PB, Full-color photos, 978-1-59473-110-5 **$8.99** *For ages 3–6*

Does God Forgive Me? *by August Gold; Full-color photos by Diane Hardy Waller*
Gently shows how God forgives all that we do if we are truly sorry.
10 x 8½, 32 pp, Quality PB, Full-color photos, 978-1-59473-142-6 **$8.99** *For ages 3–6*

God Said Amen *by Sandy Eisenberg Sasso; Full-color illus. by Avi Katz*
A warm and inspiring tale of two kingdoms that shows us that we need only reach out to each other to find the answers to our prayers.
9 x 12, 32 pp, HC, Full-color illus., 978-1-58023-080-3 **$16.95**
For ages 4 & up (A book from Jewish Lights, SkyLight Paths' sister imprint)

How Does God Listen? *by Kay Lindahl; Full-color photos by Cynthia Maloney*
How do we know when God is listening to us? Children will find the answers to these questions as they engage their senses while the story unfolds, learning how God listens in the wind, waves, clouds, hot chocolate, perfume, our tears and our laughter.
10 x 8½, 32 pp, Quality PB, Full-color photos, 978-1-59473-084-9 **$8.99** *For ages 3–6*

In God's Hands *by Lawrence Kushner and Gary Schmidt; Full-color illus. by Matthew J. Baeck*
9 x 12, 32 pp, Full-color illus., HC, 978-1-58023-224-1 **$16.99** *For ages 5 & up (A book from Jewish Lights, SkyLight Paths' sister imprint)*

In God's Name *by Sandy Eisenberg Sasso; Full-color illus. by Phoebe Stone*
Like an ancient myth in its poetic text and vibrant illustrations, this award-winning modern fable about the search for God's name celebrates the diversity and, at the same time, the unity of all the people of the world.
9 x 12, 32 pp, HC, Full-color illus., 978-1-879045-26-2 **$16.99**
For ages 4 & up (A book from Jewish Lights, SkyLight Paths' sister imprint)

Also available in Spanish: **El nombre de Dios**
9 x 12, 32 pp, HC, Full-color illus., 978-1-893361-63-8 **$16.95**

In Our Image: God's First Creatures
by Nancy Sohn Swartz; Full-color illus. by Melanie Hall
A playful new twist on the Genesis story—from the perspective of the animals. Celebrates the interconnectedness of nature and the harmony of all living things.
9 x 12, 32 pp, HC, Full-color illus., 978-1-879045-99-6 **$16.95**
For ages 4 & up (A book from Jewish Lights, SkyLight Paths' sister imprint)

Noah's Wife: The Story of Naamah
by Sandy Eisenberg Sasso; Full-color illus. by Bethanne Andersen
This new story, based on an ancient text, opens readers' religious imaginations to new ideas about the well-known story of the Flood. When God tells Noah to bring the animals of the world onto the ark, God also calls on Naamah, Noah's wife, to save each plant on Earth.
9 x 12, 32 pp, HC, Full-color illus., 978-1-58023-134-3 **$16.95**
For ages 4 & up (A book from Jewish Lights, SkyLight Paths' sister imprint)

Also available: **Naamah:** Noah's Wife (A Board Book)
by Sandy Eisenberg Sasso; Full-color illus. by Bethanne Andersen
5 x 5, 24 pp, Board Book, Full-color illus., 978-1-893361-56-0 **$7.99** *For ages 0–4*

Where Does God Live? *by August Gold and Matthew J. Perlman*
Using simple, everyday examples that children can relate to, this colorful book helps young readers develop a personal understanding of God.
10 x 8½, 32 pp, Quality PB, Full-color photo illus., 978-1-893361-39-3 **$8.99** *For ages 3–6*

Spiritual Biography / Reference

Hearing the Call across Traditions
Readings on Faith and Service
Edited by Adam Davis; Foreword by Eboo Patel
Explores the connections between faith, service, and social justice through the prose, verse, and sacred texts of the world's great faith traditions.
6 x 9, 352 pp, HC, 978-1-59473-264-5 **$29.99**

Spiritual Leaders Who Changed the World
The Essential Handbook to the Past Century of Religion
Edited by Ira Rifkin and the Editors at SkyLight Paths; Foreword by Dr. Robert Coles
An invaluable reference to the most important spiritual leaders of the past 100 years.
6 x 9, 304 pp, 15+ b/w photos, Quality PB, 978-1-59473-241-6 **$18.99**

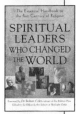

Spiritual Biography—SkyLight Lives

SkyLight Lives reintroduces the lives and works of key spiritual figures of our time—people who by their teaching or example have challenged our assumptions about spirituality and have caused us to look at it in new ways.

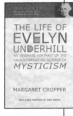

The Life of Evelyn Underhill
An Intimate Portrait of the Groundbreaking Author of Mysticism
by Margaret Cropper; Foreword by Dana Greene
Evelyn Underhill was a passionate writer and teacher who wrote elegantly on mysticism, worship, and devotional life.
6 x 9, 288 pp, 5 b/w photos, Quality PB, 978-1-893361-70-6 **$18.95**

Mahatma Gandhi: His Life and Ideas
by Charles F. Andrews; Foreword by Dr. Arun Gandhi
Examines from a contemporary Christian activist's point of view the religious ideas and political dynamics that influenced the birth of the peaceful resistance movement.
6 x 9, 336 pp, 5 b/w photos, Quality PB, 978-1-893361-89-8 **$18.95**

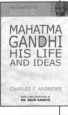

Simone Weil: A Modern Pilgrimage
by Robert Coles
The extraordinary life of the spiritual philosopher who's been called both saint and madwoman.
6 x 9, 208 pp, Quality PB, 978-1-893361-34-8 **$16.95**

Zen Effects: The Life of Alan Watts
by Monica Furlong
Through his widely popular books and lectures, Alan Watts (1915–1973) did more to introduce Eastern philosophy and religion to Western minds than any figure before or since.
6 x 9, 264 pp, Quality PB, 978-1-893361-32-4 **$16.95**

More Spiritual Biography

Bede Griffiths: An Introduction to His Interspiritual Thought
by Wayne Teasdale
The first study of his contemplative experience and thought, exploring the intersection of Hinduism and Christianity.
6 x 9, 288 pp, Quality PB, 978-1-893361-77-5 **$18.95**

The Soul of the Story: Meetings with Remarkable People
by Rabbi David Zeller
Inspiring and entertaining, this compelling collection of spiritual adventures assures us that no spiritual lesson truly learned is ever lost.
6 x 9, 288 pp, HC, 978-1-58023-272-2 **$21.99**
(A book from Jewish Lights, SkyLight Paths' sister imprint)

Prayer / Meditation

Sacred Attention: A Spiritual Practice for Finding God in the Moment
by Margaret D. McGee
Framed on the Christian liturgical year, this inspiring guide explores ways to develop a practice of attention as a means of talking—and listening—to God.
6 x 9, 144 pp, HC, 978-1-59473-232-4 **$19.99**

Women Pray: Voices through the Ages, from Many Faiths, Cultures and Traditions
Edited and with Introductions by Monica Furlong
5 x 7¼, 256 pp, Quality PB, 978-1-59473-071-9 **$15.99**

Women of Color Pray: Voices of Strength, Faith, Healing, Hope and Courage *Edited and with Introductions by Christal M. Jackson*
Through these prayers, poetry, lyrics, meditations and affirmations, you will share in the strong and undeniable connection women of color share with God.
5 x 7¼, 208 pp, Quality PB, 978-1-59473-077-1 **$15.99**

Secrets of Prayer: A Multifaith Guide to Creating Personal Prayer in Your Life *by Nancy Corcoran, CSJ*
This compelling, multifaith guidebook offers you companionship and encouragement on the journey to a healthy prayer life. 6 x 9, 160 pp, Quality PB, 978-1-59473-215-7 **$16.99**

Prayers to an Evolutionary God
by William Cleary; Afterword by Diarmuid O'Murchu
Inspired by the spiritual and scientific teachings of Diarmuid O'Murchu and Teilhard de Chardin, reveals that religion and science can be combined to create an expanding view of the universe—an evolutionary faith.
6 x 9, 208 pp, HC, 978-1-59473-006-1 **$21.99**

The Art of Public Prayer: Not for Clergy Only *by Lawrence A. Hoffman*
6 x 9, 288 pp, Quality PB, 978-1-893361-06-5 **$18.99**

A Heart of Stillness: A Complete Guide to Learning the Art of Meditation
by David A. Cooper 5½ x 8½, 272 pp, Quality PB, 978-1-893361-03-4 **$16.95**

Meditation without Gurus: A Guide to the Heart of Practice
by Clark Strand 5½ x 8½, 192 pp, Quality PB, 978-1-893361-93-5 **$16.95**

Praying with Our Hands: 21 Practices of Embodied Prayer from the World's Spiritual Traditions *by Jon M. Sweeney; Photographs by Jennifer J. Wilson; Foreword by Mother Tessa Bielecki; Afterword by Taitetsu Unno, PhD*
8 x 8, 96 pp, 22 duotone photos, Quality PB, 978-1-893361-16-4 **$16.95**

Silence, Simplicity & Solitude: A Complete Guide to Spiritual Retreat at Home
by David A. Cooper 5½ x 8½, 336 pp, Quality PB, 978-1-893361-04-1 **$16.95**

Three Gates to Meditation Practice: A Personal Journey into Sufism, Buddhism, and Judaism *by David A. Cooper* 5½ x 8½, 240 pp, Quality PB, 978-1-893361-22-5 **$16.95**

Prayer / M. Basil Pennington, OCSO

Finding Grace at the Center, 3rd Ed.: The Beginning of Centering Prayer *with Thomas Keating, OCSO, and Thomas E. Clarke, SJ; Foreword by Rev. Cynthia Bourgeault, PhD*
A practical guide to a simple and beautiful form of meditative prayer.
5 x 7¼, 128 pp, Quality PB, 978-1-59473-182-2 **$12.99**

The Monks of Mount Athos: A Western Monk's Extraordinary Spiritual Journey on Eastern Holy Ground *Foreword by Archimandrite Dionysios*
Explores the landscape, the monastic communities, and the food of Athos.
6 x 9, 256 pp, 10+ b/w drawings, Quality PB, 978-1-893361-78-2 **$18.95**

Psalms: A Spiritual Commentary *Illustrations by Phillip Ratner*
Reflections on some of the most beloved passages from the Bible's most widely read book. 6 x 9, 176 pp, 24 full-page b/w illus., Quality PB, 978-1-59473-234-8 **$16.99**
HC, 978-1-59473-141-9 **$19.99**

The Song of Songs: A Spiritual Commentary *Illustrations by Phillip Ratner*
Explore the Bible's most challenging mystical text.
6 x 9, 160 pp, 14 b/w illus., Quality PB, 978-1-59473-235-3 **$16.99**; HC, 978-1-59473-004-7 **$19.99**

Spirituality of the Seasons

Autumn: A Spiritual Biography of the Season
Edited by Gary Schmidt and Susan M. Felch; Illustrations by Mary Azarian
Rejoice in autumn as a time of preparation and reflection. Includes Wendell Berry, David James Duncan, Robert Frost, A. Bartlett Giamatti, E. B. White, P. D. James, Julian of Norwich, Garret Keizer, Tracy Kidder, Anne Lamott, May Sarton.
6 x 9, 320 pp, 5 b/w illus., Quality PB, 978-1-59473-118-1 **$18.99**

Spring: A Spiritual Biography of the Season
Edited by Gary Schmidt and Susan M. Felch; Illustrations by Mary Azarian
Explore the gentle unfurling of spring and reflect on how nature celebrates rebirth and renewal. Includes Jane Kenyon, Lucy Larcom, Harry Thurston, Nathaniel Hawthorne, Noel Perrin, Annie Dillard, Martha Ballard, Barbara Kingsolver, Dorothy Wordsworth, Donald Hall, David Brill, Lionel Basney, Isak Dinesen, Paul Laurence Dunbar. 6 x 9, 352 pp, 6 b/w illus., Quality PB, 978-1-59473-246-1 **$18.99**

Summer: A Spiritual Biography of the Season
Edited by Gary Schmidt and Susan M. Felch; Illustrations by Barry Moser
"A sumptuous banquet.... These selections lift up an exquisite wholeness found within an everyday sophistication."— ★ *Publishers Weekly* starred review
Includes Anne Lamott, Luci Shaw, Ray Bradbury, Richard Selzer, Thomas Lynch, Walt Whitman, Carl Sandburg, Sherman Alexie, Madeleine L'Engle, Jamaica Kincaid.
6 x 9, 304 pp, 5 b/w illus., Quality PB, 978-1-59473-183-9 **$18.99**
HC, 978-1-59473-083-2 **$21.99**

Winter: A Spiritual Biography of the Season
Edited by Gary Schmidt and Susan M. Felch; Illustrations by Barry Moser
"This outstanding anthology features top-flight nature and spirituality writers on the fierce, inexorable season of winter.... Remarkably lively and warm, despite the icy subject." — ★ *Publishers Weekly* starred review
Includes Will Campbell, Rachel Carson, Annie Dillard, Donald Hall, Ron Hansen, Jane Kenyon, Jamaica Kincaid, Barry Lopez, Kathleen Norris, John Updike, E. B. White.
6 x 9, 288 pp, 6 b/w illus., Deluxe PB w/flaps, 978-1-893361-92-8 **$18.95**

Spirituality / Animal Companions

Blessing the Animals: Prayers and Ceremonies to Celebrate God's Creatures, Wild and Tame *Edited by Lynn L. Caruso*
5¼ x 7¼, 256 pp, Quality PB, 978-1-59473-253-9 **$15.99**; HC, 978-1-59473-145-7 **$19.99**

Remembering My Pet: A Kid's Own Spiritual Workbook for When a Pet Dies
by Nechama Liss-Levinson, PhD, and Rev. Molly Phinney Baskette, MDiv; Foreword by Lynn L. Caruso
8 x 10, 48 pp, 2-color text, HC, 978-1-59473-221-3 **$16.99**

What Animals Can Teach Us about Spirituality: Inspiring Lessons from Wild and Tame Creatures *by Diana L. Guerrero* 6 x 9, 176 pp, Quality PB, 978-1-893361-84-3 **$16.95**

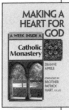

Spirituality—A Week Inside

Come and Sit: A Week Inside Meditation Centers
by Marcia Z. Nelson; Foreword by Wayne Teasdale
6 x 9, 224 pp, b/w photos, Quality PB, 978-1-893361-35-5 **$16.95**

Lighting the Lamp of Wisdom: A Week Inside a Yoga Ashram
by John Ittner; Foreword by Dr. David Frawley
6 x 9, 192 pp, 10+ b/w photos, Quality PB, 978-1-893361-52-2 **$15.95**

Making a Heart for God: A Week Inside a Catholic Monastery
by Dianne Aprile; Foreword by Brother Patrick Hart, OCSO
6 x 9, 224 pp, b/w photos, Quality PB, 978-1-893361-49-2 **$16.95**

Waking Up: A Week Inside a Zen Monastery
by Jack Maguire; Foreword by John Daido Loori, Roshi
6 x 9, 224 pp, b/w photos, Quality PB, 978-1-893361-55-3 **$16.95**; HC, 978-1-893361-13-3 **$21.95**

Spirituality

Claiming Earth as Common Ground: The Ecological Crisis through the Lens of Faith *by Andrea Cohen-Kiener; Foreword by Rev. Sally Bingham*
Inspires us to work across denominational lines in order to fulfill our sacred imperative to care for God's creation. 6 x 9, 192 pp, Quality PB, 978-1-59473-261-4 **$16.99**

The Losses of Our Lives: The Sacred Gifts of Renewal in Everyday Loss *by Dr. Nancy Copeland-Payton*
Reframes loss from the perspective that our everyday losses help us learn what we need to handle the major losses. 6 x 9, 176 pp (est), HC, 978-1-59473-271-3 **$19.99**

The Workplace and Spirituality: New Perspectives on Research and Practice *Edited by Dr. Joan Marques, Dr. Satinder Dhiman and Dr. Richard King*
Explores the benefits of workplace spirituality in making work more meaningful and rewarding. 6 x 9, 256 pp, HC, 978-1-59473-260-7 **$29.99**

A Spirituality for Brokenness: Discovering Your Deepest Self in Difficult Times *by Terry Taylor*
Guides you through a compassionate yet highly practical process of facing, accepting, and finally integrating your brokenness into your life—a process that can ultimately bring mending. 6 x 9, 176 pp, Quality PB, 978-1-59473-229-4 **$16.99**

Next to Godliness: Finding the Sacred in Housekeeping
Edited and with Introductions by Alice Peck
Offers new perspectives on how we can reach out for the Divine.
6 x 9, 224 pp, Quality PB, 978-1-59473-214-0 **$19.99**

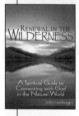

Bread, Body, Spirit: Finding the Sacred in Food
Edited and with Introductions by Alice Peck
Explores how food feeds our faith. 6 x 9, 224 pp, Quality PB, 978-1-59473-242-3 **$19.99**

Renewal in the Wilderness: A Spiritual Guide to Connecting with God in the Natural World *by John Lionberger*
Reveals the power of experiencing God's presence in many variations of the natural world. 6 x 9, 176 pp, b/w photos, Quality PB, 978-1-59473-219-5 **$16.99**

Honoring Motherhood: Prayers, Ceremonies and Blessings
Edited and with Introductions by Lynn L. Caruso
Journey through the seasons of motherhood. 5 x 7¼, 272 pp, HC, 978-1-59473-239-3 **$19.99**

Soul Fire: Accessing Your Creativity *by Rev. Thomas Ryan, CSP*
Learn to cultivate your creative spirit. 6 x 9, 160 pp, Quality PB, 978-1-59473-243-0 **$16.99**

Money and the Way of Wisdom: Insights from the Book of Proverbs
by Timothy J. Sandoval, PhD 6 x 9, 192 pp, Quality PB, 978-1-59473-245-4 **$16.99**

Creating a Spiritual Retirement: A Guide to the Unseen Possibilities in Our Lives
by Molly Srode 6 x 9, 208 pp, b/w photos, Quality PB, 978-1-59473-050-4 **$14.99**
HC, 978-1-893361-75-1 **$19.95**

Finding Hope: Cultivating God's Gift of a Hopeful Spirit
by Marcia Ford 8 x 8, 200 pp, Quality PB, 978-1-59473-211-9 **$16.99**

Jewish Spirituality: A Brief Introduction for Christians *by Lawrence Kushner*
5½ x 8½, 112 pp, Quality PB, 978-1-58023-150-3 **$12.95** *(A book from Jewish Lights, SkyLight Paths' sister imprint)*

Journeys of Simplicity: Traveling Light with Thomas Merton, Bashō, Edward Abbey, Annie Dillard & Others *by Philip Harnden*
5 x 7¼, 144 pp, Quality PB, 978-1-59473-181-5 **$12.99** 128 pp, HC, 978-1-893361-76-8 **$16.95**

Keeping Spiritual Balance As We Grow Older: More than 65 Creative Ways to Use Purpose, Prayer, and the Power of Spirit to Build a Meaningful Retirement
by Molly and Bernie Srode 8 x 8, 224 pp, Quality PB, 978-1-59473-042-9 **$16.99**

Spiritually Incorrect: Finding God in All the Wrong Places *by Dan Wakefield; Illus. by Marian DelVecchio* 5½ x 8½, 192 pp, b/w illus., Quality PB, 978-1-59473-137-2 **$15.99**

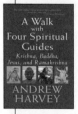

A Walk with Four Spiritual Guides: Krishna, Buddha, Jesus, and Ramakrishna
by Andrew Harvey 5½ x 8½, 192 pp, 10 b/w photos & illus., Quality PB, 978-1-59473-138-9 **$15.99**

Spirituality & Crafts

Beading—The Creative Spirit: Finding Your Sacred Center through the Art of Beadwork *by Rev. Wendy Ellsworth*
Invites you on a spiritual pilgrimage into the kaleidoscope world of glass and color.   7 x 9, 240 pp, 8-page full-color insert, plus b/w photographs and diagrams
Quality PB, 978-1-59473-267-6 **$18.99**

Contemplative Crochet: A Hands-On Guide for Interlocking Faith and Craft *by Cindy Crandall-Frazier; Foreword by Linda Skolnik*
Illuminates the spiritual lessons you can learn through crocheting.
7 x 9, 208 pp, b/w photographs, Quality PB, 978-1-59473-238-6 **$16.99**

The Knitting Way: A Guide to Spiritual Self-Discovery
by Linda Skolnik and Janice MacDaniels Examines how you can explore and strengthen your spiritual life through knitting.
7 x 9, 240 pp, b/w photographs Quality PB, 978-1-59473-079-5 **$16.99**

The Painting Path: Embodying Spiritual Discovery through Yoga, Brush and Color *by Linda Novick; Foreword by Richard Segalman*
Explores the divine connection you can experience through creativity.
7 x 9, 208 pp, 8-page full-color insert, plus b/w photographs
Quality PB, 978-1-59473-226-3 **$18.99**

The Quilting Path: A Guide to Spiritual Discovery through Fabric, Thread and Kabbalah *by Louise Silk*
Explores how to cultivate personal growth through quilt making.
7 x 9, 192 pp, b/w photographs and illustrations, Quality PB, 978-1-59473-206-5 **$16.99**

The Scrapbooking Journey: A Hands-On Guide to Spiritual Discovery
by Cory Richardson-Lauve; Foreword by Stacy Julian Reveals how this craft can become a practice used to deepen and shape your life.
7 x 9, 176 pp, 8-page full-color insert, plus b/w photographs, Quality PB, 978-1-59473-216-4 **$18.99**

The Soulwork of Clay: A Hands-On Approach to Spirituality
by Marjory Zoet Bankson; Photographs by Peter Bankson
Takes you through the seven-step process of making clay into a pot, drawing parallels at each stage to the process of spiritual growth.
7 x 9, 192 pp, b/w photographs, Quality PB, 978-1-59473-249-2 **$16.99**

Kabbalah / Enneagram
(Books from Jewish Lights Publishing, SkyLight Paths' sister imprint)

God in Your Body: Kabbalah, Mindfulness and Embodied Spiritual Practice
by Jay Michaelson 6 x 9, 288 pp, Quality PB Original, 978-1-58023-304-0 **$18.99**

Cast in God's Image: Discover Your Personality Type Using the Enneagram and Kabbalah
by Rabbi Howard A. Addison 7 x 9, 176 pp, Quality PB, 978-1-58023-124-4 **$16.95**

Ehyeh: A Kabbalah for Tomorrow *by Dr. Arthur Green*
6 x 9, 224 pp, Quality PB, 978-1-58023-213-5 **$16.99**

The Enneagram and Kabbalah, 2nd Edition: Reading Your Soul
by Rabbi Howard A. Addison 6 x 9, 192 pp, Quality PB, 978-1-58023-229-6 **$16.99**

The Gift of Kabbalah: Discovering the Secrets of Heaven, Renewing Your Life on Earth
by Tamar Frankiel, PhD 6 x 9, 256 pp, Quality PB, 978-1-58023-141-1 **$16.95**
HC, 978-1-58023-108-4 **$21.95**

Kabbalah: A Brief Introduction for Christians
by Tamar Frankiel, PhD 5½ x 8¼, 176 pp, Quality PB, 978-1-58023-303-3 **$16.99**

Zohar: Annotated & Explained *Translation and Annotation by Dr. Daniel C. Matt*
Foreword by Andrew Harvey 5½ x 8¼, 176 pp, Quality PB, 978-1-893361-51-5 **$15.99**
(A book from Jewish Lights, SkyLight Paths' sister imprint)

Spiritual Practice

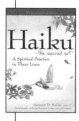

Haiku—The Sacred Art: A Spiritual Practice in Three Lines
by Margaret D. McGee Introduces haiku as a simple and effective way of tapping into the sacred moments that permeate everyday living.
5½ x 8½, 160 pp (est), Quality PB, 978-1-59473-269-0 **$16.99**

Dance—The Sacred Art: The Joy of Movement as a Spiritual Practice
by Cynthia Winton-Henry Invites all of us, regardless of experience, into the possibility of dance/movement as a spiritual practice.
5½ x 8½, 160 pp (est), Quality PB, 978-1-59473-268-3 **$16.99**

Spiritual Adventures in the Snow: Skiing & Snowboarding as Renewal for Your Soul *by Dr. Marcia McFee and Rev. Karen Foster; Foreword by Paul Arthur*
Explores snow sports as tangible experiences of the spiritual essence of our bodies and the earth. 5½ x 8½, 160 pp (est), Quality PB, 978-1-59473-270-6 **$16.99**

Recovery—The Sacred Art: The Twelve Steps as Spiritual Practice
by Rami Shapiro; Foreword by Joan Borysenko, PhD Uniquely interprets the Twelve Steps of Alcoholics Anonymous to speak to everyone seeking a freer and more God-centered life. 5½ x 8½, 240 pp, Quality PB, 978-1-59473-259-1 **$16.99**

Soul Fire: Accessing Your Creativity *by Rev. Thomas Ryan, CSP*
Shows you how to cultivate your creative spirit as a way to encourage personal growth.
6 x 9, 160 pp, Quality PB, 978-1-59473-243-0 **$16.99**

Running—The Sacred Art: Preparing to Practice
by Dr. Warren A. Kay; Foreword by Kristin Armstrong Examines how your daily run can enrich your spiritual life. 5½ x 8½, 160 pp, Quality PB, 978-1-59473-227-0 **$16.99**

Hospitality—The Sacred Art: Discovering the Hidden Spiritual Power of Invitation and Welcome *by Rev. Nanette Sawyer; Foreword by Rev. Dirk Ficca*
5½ x 8½, 192 pp, Quality PB, 978-1-59473-228-7 **$16.99**

Thanking & Blessing—The Sacred Art: Spiritual Vitality through Gratefulness
by Jay Marshall, PhD; Foreword by Philip Gulley 5½ x 8½, 176 pp, Quality PB, 978-1-59473-231-7 **$16.99**

Everyday Herbs in Spiritual Life: A Guide to Many Practices
by Michael J. Caduto; Foreword by Rosemary Gladstar
7 x 9, 208 pp, 21 b/w illustrations, Quality PB, 978-1-59473-174-7 **$16.99**

Divining the Body: Reclaim the Holiness of Your Physical Self *by Jan Phillips*
8 x 8, 256 pp, Quality PB, 978-1-59473-080-1 **$16.99**

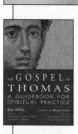

The Gospel of Thomas: A Guidebook for Spiritual Practice
by Ron Miller; Translations by Stevan Davies 6 x 9, 160 pp, Quality PB, 978-1-59473-047-4 **$14.99**

Labyrinths from the Outside In: Walking to Spiritual Insight—A Beginner's Guide
by Donna Schaper and Carole Ann Camp
6 x 9, 208 pp, b/w illus. and photos, Quality PB, 978-1-893361-18-8 **$16.95**

Practicing the Sacred Art of Listening: A Guide to Enrich Your Relationships and Kindle Your Spiritual Life *by Kay Lindahl* 8 x 8, 176 pp, Quality PB, 978-1-893361-85-0 **$16.95**

The Sacred Art of Bowing: Preparing to Practice
by Andi Young 5½ x 8½, 128 pp, b/w illus., Quality PB, 978-1-893361-82-9 **$14.95**

The Sacred Art of Chant: Preparing to Practice
by Ana Hernández 5½ x 8½, 192 pp, Quality PB, 978-1-59473-036-8 **$15.99**

The Sacred Art of Fasting: Preparing to Practice
by Thomas Ryan, CSP 5½ x 8½, 192 pp, Quality PB, 978-1-59473-078-8 **$15.99**

The Sacred Art of Forgiveness: Forgiving Ourselves and Others through God's Grace
by Marcia Ford 8 x 8, 176 pp, Quality PB, 978-1-59473-175-4 **$16.99**

The Sacred Art of Listening: Forty Reflections for Cultivating a Spiritual Practice
by Kay Lindahl; Illustrations by Amy Schnapper
8 x 8, 160 pp, b/w illus., Quality PB, 978-1-893361-44-7 **$16.99**

The Sacred Art of Lovingkindness: Preparing to Practice
by Rabbi Rami Shapiro; Foreword by Marcia Ford 5½ x 8½, 176 pp, Quality PB, 978-1-59473-151-8 **$16.99**

Sacred Speech: A Practical Guide for Keeping Spirit in Your Speech
by Rev. Donna Schaper 6 x 9, 176 pp, Quality PB, 978-1-59473-068-9 **$15.99**
HC, 978-1-893361-74-4 **$21.95**

Spiritual Poetry—The Mystic Poets

Experience these mystic poets as you never have before. Each beautiful, compact book includes: a brief introduction to the poet's time and place; a summary of the major themes of the poet's mysticism and religious tradition; essential selections from the poet's most important works; and an appreciative preface by a contemporary spiritual writer.

Hafiz
The Mystic Poets
Preface by Ibrahim Gamard
Hafiz is known throughout the world as Persia's greatest poet, with sales of his poems in Iran today only surpassed by those of the Qur'an itself. His probing and joyful verse speaks to people from all backgrounds who long to taste and feel divine love and experience harmony with all living things.
5 x 7¼, 144 pp, HC, 978-1-59473-009-2 **$16.99**

Hopkins
The Mystic Poets
Preface by Rev. Thomas Ryan, CSP
Gerard Manley Hopkins, Christian mystical poet, is beloved for his use of fresh language and startling metaphors to describe the world around him. Although his verse is lovely, beneath the surface lies a searching soul, wrestling with and yearning for God.
5 x 7¼, 112 pp, HC, 978-1-59473-010-8 **$16.99**

Tagore
The Mystic Poets
Preface by Swami Adiswarananda
Rabindranath Tagore is often considered the "Shakespeare" of modern India. A great mystic, Tagore was the teacher of W. B. Yeats and Robert Frost, the close friend of Albert Einstein and Mahatma Gandhi, and the winner of the Nobel Prize for Literature. This beautiful sampling of Tagore's two most important works, *The Gardener* and *Gitanjali*, offers a glimpse into his spiritual vision that has inspired people around the world.
5 x 7¼, 144 pp, HC, 978-1-59473-008-5 **$16.99**

Whitman
The Mystic Poets
Preface by Gary David Comstock
Walt Whitman was the most innovative and influential poet of the nineteenth century. This beautiful sampling of Whitman's most important poetry from *Leaves of Grass*, and selections from his prose writings, offers a glimpse into the spiritual side of his most radical themes—love for country, love for others, and love of Self.
5 x 7¼, 192 pp, HC, 978-1-59473-041-2 **$16.99**

Journeys of Simplicity
Traveling Light with Thomas Merton, Bashō, Edward Abbey, Annie Dillard & Others
Invites you to consider a more graceful way of traveling through life. Use the included journal pages (in PB only) to help you get started on your own spiritual journey.

by Philip Harnden
5 x 7¼, 144 pp, Quality PB, 978-1-59473-181-5 **$12.99**
128 pp, HC, 978-1-893361-76-8 **$16.95**

About SKYLIGHT PATHS Publishing

SkyLight Paths Publishing is creating a place where people of different spiritual traditions come together for challenge and inspiration, a place where we can help each other understand the mystery that lies at the heart of our existence.

Through spirituality, our religious beliefs are increasingly becoming a part of our lives—rather than *apart* from our lives. While many of us may be more interested than ever in spiritual growth, we may be less firmly planted in traditional religion. Yet, we do want to deepen our relationship to the sacred, to learn from our own as well as from other faith traditions, and to practice in new ways.

SkyLight Paths sees both believers and seekers as a community that increasingly transcends traditional boundaries of religion and denomination—people wanting to learn from each other, *walking together, finding the way.*

For your information and convenience, at the back of this book we have provided a list of other SkyLight Paths books you might find interesting and useful. They cover the following subjects:

Buddhism / Zen	Global Spiritual	Monasticism
Catholicism	Perspectives	Mysticism
Children's Books	Gnosticism	Poetry
Christianity	Hinduism /	Prayer
Comparative	Vedanta	Religious Etiquette
Religion	Inspiration	Retirement
Current Events	Islam / Sufism	Spiritual Biography
Earth-Based	Judaism	Spiritual Direction
Spirituality	Kabbalah	Spirituality
Enneagram	Meditation	Women's Interest
	Midrash Fiction	Worship

Or phone, fax, mail or e-mail to: SKYLIGHT PATHS Publishing
Sunset Farm Offices, Route 4 • P.O. Box 237 • Woodstock, Vermont 05091
Tel: (802) 457-4000 • Fax: (802) 457-4004 • www.skylightpaths.com
Credit card orders: (800) 962-4544 (8:30AM–5:30PM ET Monday–Friday)
Generous discounts on quantity orders. SATISFACTION GUARANTEED. Prices subject to change.